LOVE POEMS AND OBSESSION

LOVE POEMS AND OBSESSION

by: Cheryl Krkoč

Title: Love Poems and Obsession
Copyright © 2021 by Cheryl Krkoč. All rights reserved.

No part of this publication may be reproduced, stored in a retrieval system or transmitted in any way by any means, electronic, mechanical, photocopy, recording or otherwise without the prior permission of the author except as provided by USA copyright law.

To order additional copies of this book:
www.amazon.com
www.barnesandnoble.com

Published in the United States of America

ISBN *hardcover: 9781956895049*
ISBN *softcover: 9781956895056*

Dedication

For Dad
The Renaissance Man

And Mom
The Quiet One

Contents

Introduction 9

Poems 15

Guestbook Beach Retreat Poems 239

Epilogue 249

Original Poems 251

Two Sided Poems 341

Photos 351

Bibliography 365

Introduction

I was aware from early on that there was a special relationship between my parents. They represented to me true love, devotion, passion, romance, conflict and mystery. But I didn't begin to grasp the depth and complicated aspects of their relationship until I came across an album that I assumed was another of the photo albums I poured over at my brother's home shortly after our mother's death in September of 2013. Dad was already gone. He died in April of 2012. I was in the middle of writing my memoir and digging through scads of photo albums and boxes of loose photos to include in the book. I called my brother and asked if I could take a look at the albums he had at his own place. When I got to his home, a few miles from my own, we explored the contents of his collection. It was then that I came across an album, not with photos, but with poetry Dad had written to Mom over the course of most of their lives together. We kids had all been aware of Dad's bent in writing little ditties now and again. Our special place at the Oregon coast contained unit diaries for guests (provided by the owners) to make entries about their experiences during their stays. Over the years these accumulated until there were many to peruse during any given stay. None were ever discarded as far as I know. With each visit, one could find entries of our family members still intact and accessible to every guest. Dad's entries were always the easiest to spot because of his very distinctive cursive, other than the owner of our favorite unit who had an eerily similar style to Dad's. Dad also proclaimed, at times, that he did write poems for Mom's pleasure, but we kids were seldom privy to them. And now, here they were, for my own pleasure-or pain, as I would have it. As I began my journey through Dad's scripture I was reminded of his propensity for deep melancholy, fits of grandiosity, and episodes of tripping the light fantastic. He could be a whirlwind, who seemed (sometimes) barely to notice anything going on outside his own experience. His poems also brought to mind Mom's inclination towards aloofness and her morbid preoccupation with resentment and guilt. And then there was her adoration of Dad, sometimes turning on a dime to abhorrence.

Now Dad was never a scholarly poet. He dedicated this aspect of his life to the sciences, resulting in a doctorate in medicine. He specialized in radiology. I think he felt that becoming a physician would somehow make up for his humble beginnings as the son of immigrants. He was convinced that the sciences were supreme in the big scheme of things, but he also had sentimental leanings towards the humanities- art, literature, philosophy, history, etc. This is what really drove him. These pursuits of his remained entirely on an amateur level-never any formal instruction or training in how to go about creating a piece of artwork, poem, or comprehending serious literature, philosophy, etc. He was innately intelligent though, and had an artist's emotional makeup, so he persevered. He dabbled in art, poetry, and the pursuit of knowledge in all the areas of the humanities.

Over the years, I always thought of myself as pretty important to Dad-always aware of his sentimentality and affection towards me. But he was always able to make just about anyone feel special while in his presence. This must have had to do with his sentimental nature, his zest for life and his charisma. However, this magic only happened with anyone he liked. Otherwise, it was a whole other ball of wax. It was not until I read through his love poems to my mother after their deaths that I realized he was entirely obsessed with her and that no one could ever come close in his heart to her. His devotion became all-consuming and in the end led to melancholy and self-doubt. I don't know how my mother felt about his devotion. His poems suggest that she was often silent about any feelings for him that she might have had. This always seemed to keep him guessing. His attempt to salve her despair seemed often to be in vain. He became unsure of himself in his relationship with her. It was apparent that he listened. He knew something of her torturous past with her family of origin so she must have confided in him at least some of the time and she confided only in him, for the most part. But Mom was a mystery to us all. I think Dad knew her better than anyone ever did but it seemed there was still much hidden, even from him.

When Dad wrote about Mom he described her as all-giving to everyone in her family. In some regard this was true. She was quiet, sensitive to other's feelings, and spent her time taking care of her family. Dad orchestrated the direction her life would take though, and so did the flavor of the era they both lived in. Mom became the consummate homemaker. Her station in the home was the kitchen-most of her time spent there turning out breakfast, lunch and dinner for whichever of us took a seat next to the kitchen island that separated this room from the family room. This is also where she ironed just about everything that came out of the dryer or from the clothes line. But then, there was also her inadvertent Angst that seemed to preclude any real ability for her to relate to her family on a deeper level. Dad may have been the only one who knew her at all.

Dad wrote poetry just about anywhere he was and on just about anything he could find-a napkin or paper place mat in whatever restaurant he visited, note pads left in his hotel room, etc. Often he wrote while alone, out of town for business or pleasure, and often feeling a little lonely-especially missing Mom. My sister Sandra remembers his writing Mom a love ditty on our refrigerator in our Ninth Street house when we kids were all still living at home. It ended with his proclamation that if she wiped away his words then "you'll be wiping away my love". Sandra remembers the poem remaining on the refrigerator for months. After her telling me this memory of hers I could recollect it myself.

I would like to share some of the poetry in the photo album, entries in the journals at our beach place, postcards and also some letters I kept that Dad wrote to Mom while he was away from home. They are for anyone who might be interested. Maybe no one, but that's O.K. too. I want to include his writings in his own hand because they bring them more to life. (My ex-husband Leo took photographs of the entries in the journals from our beach retreat so they too are in Dad's own hand). I will also include a typed version because sometimes his cursive is difficult to decipher and his writing materials were not always conducive to a clear read either. Dad's first language was Slovenian. He didn't learn English until he started the first grade. He went on in school for years to get a doctorate but in his writing, at least with his poetry, he often misspelled words. Sometimes his spellings seemed to have been intentional. He often combined two different words to make one so that his coined word could represent two different meanings at once. I don't know if his slow start with the English language left him at a disadvantage or if he just was more preoccupied with the meaning of the words he was writing. His miss-spellings, more often than not, were done phonetically. In doing my research for my memoir about Slovenija, I found that the Slovenian language is conducive to creative and powerful poetry. There are many poets in the country known for the beautiful poems they have created in this ancient language. Maybe somehow, Dad was able to tap into this energy because of both his inherent and actual knowledge of the language. Having access to these writings of his have been very meaningful to me-even more so because towards the end of his life he was unable to speak at all. The course of his loss of speech was gradual but relentless.

I found myself in the role of sleuth while working on this project. The meaning of his poems required me to go back in time and relive our life events as a family. Reading them also brought back intimate conversations Dad and I had over the years that helped me to understand and decipher each poem's meaning. I cannot say that my interpretation is always accurate but I think I understood Dad more than just about anyone. I will be using brackets to add or change his poem to make it more understandable to the reader- such as adding commas, etc., spelling misspelled words or clarifying his intentions to the best of my ability.

Dad had a sapient nature and, in his later years, had the goal of learning every word in his dictionary. I would observe him in his easy chair scanning each page. Sometimes he would share with others a word he learned that he hadn't known about before. I wonder if his knowledge of three different languages contributed to his interest in this endeavor. I also wonder if his first language, Slovenian, left him with something of an advantage in creating unique combinations of meaning and form in his writing that I have found unique. His interest wasn't confined to English though. He studied books that were in and about Yiddish, German, Slovenian, and Italian.

Poems

To A Wife

The first poem in the album wasn't dated. In fact, many of the earlier poems weren't. However, this first of Dad's love poems to Mom included a long-stemmed rose attached to the left of his cursive, written on a small notebook lined page and above it was a photo of himself in his sailor suit and hat. This indicates to me that the poem was written early on, probably shortly after their marriage. It reads as follows:

To a wife
Sweet love
like death's kiss
has devoured me
and placed me
on your lips.
A Husband

Even early on, it seemed that Dad expressed the darker side of his affection, for he likens his "sweet love" to "death's kiss"- abandonment of his own destiny and some of his own annihilation. His wife's love had "devoured" him. She has taken him into herself, even if unintentionally. But then she "placed" [him] on [her] lips- which does imply intention on her part-but something that he seems to accept. At its end, he signs the poem "A Husband"- defining himself in relation to her-a simple poem by comparison, but a start.

It's Odd

It ['] s odd how can it be

the strange peace your presence brings [to] me

In content I sit silently

my life passing pleasantly

Yes odd how can it be

Why should your presence do

this to me

As I sit silently.

Heart and mind alone won[']t tell

For time and time alone

In this second poem of the collection Dad writes of a "strange peace" that his lover's presence brings him. The word "strange" may suggest that her influence is difficult for him to understand, and maybe even incomprehensible. The third and fourth lines find him "content" in her presence though-so much so that he doesn't have to say a word but feels his passing (a finite concept, it seems) "pleasantly"-similar (maybe) to his prior reference to the peace her presence brings him and also to "passing"-to a final fatal end that cannot be avoided. Is she going to lead to his demise? Is she a femme fatal? In the next three lines, he questions her having such an influence over his well-being, and the last two lines tell us that neither his heart nor his mind can answer this question, but maybe only, at some point in the future, it may be made clear to him.

When Alone

#1

When alone it ['] s easy to dream

and live in fantasy how

you will fight to save your
lover from impending tragedy
Yet in reality
More honest deeds requiring
greater bravery can be–
to give your life to one
who only loves you in return
then recall the price men
pay to pride and jelousy [jealousy]
and before you fall all acts of bravery.
True love lives in the hearts of men
not tongues of hipocrits [hypocrites] who leave
the battle to enemies
as pride and jelousy [jealousy]
which soon devour the keeper
for he can never set them free.
#2
Understanding is
a Simple deed
a Simple act
Ah!
True love
in fact.
#3 (corny)
Hide from life
It can be done
But Death
is never out run.

This poem is in parts-1,2,3. In #1 the first four lines seem to address the fanciful nature of daydreaming about being a protector of one's lover from "impending tragedy". I wonder what sort of tragedy is he referring to? Is it another with intent to harm? Or is it his lover's own demons? The next five lines-instead of "fighting" off negative external or internal influences for his lover, there is personal "bravery" found in one's dedication to the one who returns his love. It takes bravery of this sort to love so completely. The final nine lines in #1 liken the emotions of "pride and jealousy" as a barrier or falling away from caring. He adds-"…recall the price men pay to pride and jealousy and before you fall all acts of bravery." This kind of bravery, related to pride and jealousy, is not noble and not really the truest bravery. Next, he states that "true love lives in hearts of men" which is likened to feelings of the heart in care of another. He then compares this to the" tongues of hipocrits [hypocrites] who leave the battle to enemies [such] as pride and jelousy [jealousy]. Pride and jealousy are enemies to caring and if one chooses this way it will "devour the keeper" [who clings to pride and jealousy], which will destroy any ability to truly love because the person who clings to these ways "can never set them [pride and jealousy] free."

#2 These six lines support part #1- simply stating that understanding is the essence of love-knowing someone through and through, simple things that demonstrate you know and care- "A simple deed/ A simple act/ Ah!" That is what it takes for "True love/in fact".

#3 Dad writes (corny) at the top of this section-maybe meant to separate it from the first two sections which complement each other and to provide his opinion of this section of the poem. "Hide from life/It can be done/ But Death/ is never outrun". I don't think it is corny. It tells the reader to live life to the fullest for death is in one's future, for sure. This is a theme that runs in many of his poems. He seemed to have a keen awareness of his mortality from an early age. I do believe that his family history marked with tragedy and loss played a part in his relationship with the topic of death, but he also mentions, just as easily, the prospect of life after death.

Flowers
Flowers for the one I love may
reveal the way my heart feels.
But my love [is] more like the
seeds unseen-implanted
[that] leads to untold multiplicity.
then each in turn again-
again to come with splendor
to unfolding.
till the odor like a taste
of love
Grows & Grows Unending.

Here is one of Dad's soliloquies. He had a habit of bringing Mom flowers as a symbol of his affection and devotion. In fact, roses were his favorites, and he planted a row along the south side of our Ninth Street home-next to a walkway he and the rest of us created shortly after his purchase of the place. It was made of slate rock from the area near Todd Lake in the Cascade Mountain Range-held together with cement. Dad starts this poem [the first two lines] describing the flowers as a means of expressing his love-"The way my heart feels." He goes on to say that his love, though, is more like the/seeds unseen-implanted/[that] leads to untold [incalculable] multiplicity./then each in turn again-/again to come with splendor [great luster or brightness]/to unfolding [making known]."-for the cut flowers perish, but the seeds he plants continue to perpetuate [preserve from oblivion] like his love for his beloved and I suspect he is also referring to the offspring that are the product of the union between them. This, in turn, results in the continuation of his love and progeny. In lines 9 and 10 of the poem he likens the "odor" [scent] of the flowers to a "taste of love"-It seems to me a sexual simile for the odor and taste of sexual intimacy, but also the scent and flower's seed that "Grows and Grows Unending"-referring again to the everlasting and eternal quality of his love. This last line has all capitalized words-another indication that he speaks of Immortality and a connection to God and the evolution of all of nature and humanity.

Dearest

Dearest, when you are near
Countless times I've pondered,
"Why not reveal what lies
here beneath your breast"?
For it seems[,] like Cerano [Cyrano,] I
Must pen my love or it
will never be told,
and I wish you to know
my heart is never still
but forever expands
like the rush of a breeze
through boughs of trees

Tenderly caressing and
kissing the leaves.

Here we have another soliloquy and it may be even more an intimate portrayal of Dad's inner workings than that of even the previous poem. He often expressed his difficulty in verbalizing his devotion to Mom. In this poem he questions his trepidation –"Why not reveal what lies here beneath your breast"? He goes on to say that the only way he seems to be able to do so is through his poetry. If not for that-"It will never be told,"-It seems a rather lonely statement, don't you think? Mom was never expressive about her own feelings until the nearing of her death. At least I rarely saw that side of her. Is this what made her mate shy about doing so? Regarding his reference to "Cerano"-the correct spelling is Cyrano [de Bergerac]-Dad identifies with the character of Cyrano in regard to his inability to profess his love openly to his amour. He can do this only through his writing because of his own insecurity about his love interest.

In the last seven lines Dad again makes reference to the everlasting nature of his devotion-likened to nature and the universe-his heart[beneath his breast] "…forever expands/ like the rush of a breeze/Through the boughs of the trees"-This breeze takes on his human sensual love making-"Tenderly caressing and kissing the leaves"-making love to the trees as he does to his beloved. He has now become a more active participant through his written words, which mimic the expanding and everlasting universe, and she is the recipient of this force of nature.

Again-Again
The strings tug at my heart

and choke back all its efforts.
Again-Again
That hollow feeling grips me
as we sit apart.
I feel your presence then, would be like-
rain drops in the desert-
a comet in the sky-
No-More like
God, to one about to die.
This vanishes-then a
voice whispers-
Can this be- One
With flesh of dust
Touched-
with things that live eternally.

This is my favorite of all of Dad's poems that I have had access to and that form some sort of uncomfortable connection to her, his Muse. There is such an expression of melancholy, even torment, in the first six lines of this poem. The affect, his sense of emotional separation from his wife is powerfully expressed in these lines-"The strings tug at my heart/and choke back all its efforts [to speak]./Again-Again/That hollow feeling grips me/ as we sit apart." His inability to reach her with words creates an emotional separation from her [as they sit apart, incommunicado] and leads to a profound loneliness-a 'hollow feeling"-almost an annihilation [to make into nothing]. In the next ten lines he finds relief from this torture when he feels her [emotional] presence, which manifests itself as "…like raindrops in the desert"-he may have perished if not for the raindrops. Or maybe, he writes, her presence is more like "a comet in the sky"-a bright presence in the darkness [his void]. He likens this awareness of her presence to natural and beautiful wonders-"raindrops" in a normally barren region; a comet lighting up a dark sky.

But even these examples do not truly portray the magnitude of what her presence means to him. He writes-"No-[she is] More like/God, to one about to die." Nothing, it seems, could be more significant than this. But then her presence takes on a new meaning altogether. His notion about her presence being "…like God, to one about to die./ …vanishes-/ [and] then a/voice whispers-" [I believe, his own voice/and or God's]-and this is when he asks himself the question-"Can this be-One [capitalized-signifying a deity?]/With flesh of dust/Touched-/with things that live eternally." He doesn't add a question mark at the end of this pondering, suggesting that he may already know the answer-that he is "…One/with flesh of dust/Touched-with things that live eternally"-again not a question at all really, but his own conviction, and a confirmation from God, that love is eternal, flesh and dust are one and the same, and he will remain with his beloved for eternity in a more perfect union than what he has found with her on earth.

Hedonistic

Here Lies

No cares

No fears

No tears

No permanent alliance

No stare

No poem
Uncherished
Completely alone

Directly under the title line "Hedonistic" he writes "Here Lies" to introduce the characteristics of the hedonist. Is he also labeling himself as such? Dad goes on to describe what he considers to be characteristics of a hedonist-void of serious emotions-cares, fears, tears, "No permanent alliance." I'm not sure about the line after. Is it "No stare"? If so, this might refer to an "intent look or gaze of admiration or wonder" (# 1, pg. 1422) of one's beloved. Then there would be "No poem" written in awe of one's beloved if the hedonist doesn't pay attention [stare- look inside] to her. The hedonist [and consequently the hedonist's love partner] will be "uncherished" by any other and "Completely alone".

His use of the word hedonist seems rather ironic to me, as Dad was, in my opinion, a hedonist-pleasure seeker- himself and he may have thought so too. But maybe he felt that going too far with the pursuit of pleasure will dampen the ability to be caring of others, to truly love and form meaningful relationships. Maybe the narcissistic quality in hedonism is what he was referring to; then he might be able to step away from the narcissitic hedonist in himself and take the role of philantropist.

Dearest One Only One
Dearest and only one
Your sweetness and ways
remain a mystery to me.
as mine may seem to you.
Like the rose on the

Vine your scent & sweetness
sublime transpose to me
a most important clime.

In this poem Dad addresses his love as the "dearest [and] only one." He describes his wife's ways as "a mystery" to him and that he doesn't understand her. Then he suggests to her that she may not understand him either-"as mine [my ways] may seem [a mystery] to you." In this poem, again, he likens her to "a rose on the vine." Again, he speaks of her "scent and sweetness sublime" which will "transpose" to him "a most important clime." A clime or climate (#2, pg. 274) is a realm [of thought] or could be a different climate from what is usual- an emotional state or a weather condition [tropical and lush, or desolate and dry/ mysterious?]-and she takes him there. The usual meaning of transpose is to change the usual order of things (#3 pg. 1549) and the word also, in an obsolete way, means to transform (#4, pgs. 1549 & 1546)-to change the condition of. Either word could convey that her essence- her "scent & sweetness"-transforms him and takes him to a different realm-of thought and emotion.

With this poem, I also reflect on my mother's very porcelain and fragile skin. She was unable to tend to or be near Dad's rose bushes, for they tore away at her flesh. I also wonder if he may have been making reference in this poem to thorns on the rose vine when he likens her to "a rose on the vine" which has the luscious scent and beautiful appearance, but also the thorns that are dangerous too-not only for his wife's skin but also her own self destructive nature and a dangerous influence over him.

Hearts Heavy [no date]
Hearts heavy but my
chest feels void.
Can't understand it.
Stare, eyes moisten then dew.
Motionless the body weeps too.
Spirit[']s gone a
thing of unquest
Found again only in rest.
Feel a patch of sunshine off to my left a bit
reach it?
Once thought I did.
Fed on its sweet substance was my everywhere
Eyes open-Oh dispair [despair,] there is darkness everywhere
Here on earth at last
With others sharing a past
Escaped so well so long
Had a happy inner song.
Such a simple tune
now gone.

This three part trilogy seems to have been written during a dark period of my father's life. There are no dates assigned to these earlier poems, so I can only guess at what might have been occurring during the time he wrote this one. The first section- "Heart's heavy"- suggests sadness but "...my/Chest feels void" seems more like an emptiness or nothingness [annihilation], but he "can't understand" why. In the fourth line, again, as in the poem Hedonist, he uses the word "stare"-maybe this time his stare is blank. But then, his "...eyes moisten, then dew"-again, sadness. The emotion goes unnoticed because his body is motionless but inside his body weeps too-as his eyes dew [do]. In the last three lines of the first part he says his "spirit[']s gone [which is] a thing of unquest"-that he feels dead need not be questioned. Unquest is the opposite of quest-to seek, a pursuit of (#6, pg. 1193). His spirit is void of motion. The only thing then that offers any solace (#7, pg. 1386/comfort) from this state is "found again only in rest" and rest seems reminiscent of death. I do remember my father's states. They were difficult to witness, but I'm sure more difficult to bear.

In the second part of the trilogy-"Feel a patch of sunshine"-there is little reprieve from the sense of hopelessness found in the first. There is a juxtaposing of light and darkness in this segment. He feels "a patch of sunshine" off to his left a bit. [Mom often sat next to him in the family room on his left. She sat closest to the window. They both had leather chairs of red]. He doesn't say he sees the sunshine but feels it only. He hasn't made a concerted effort to look in its direction, only senses the light's presence based on the warmth. Did he think he feels the sunshine's warmth or that emanating from her? He asks himself if he can reach it and answers himself-"once thought I did." He remembers that he "fed on its sweet substance [the real or essential part or element of anything; essence] (#8, pg. 1454) [and it] was my everywhere". Instead of everything he uses everywhere, I think, because when he was able to feel her essence it would be with him wherever he was-in or out of her actual presence. But now, when he opens his eyes [becomes aware] the light is gone and there is "…darkness everywhere"-in spite of his having his eyes wide open. She is gone, the light is gone, and he despairs. I remember Mom telling me that she fell out of love for my father and that she had to pray to get it back. I have wondered if there ever was a full recovery of this love on her part.

In the third part-"Here on earth"-Dad reminisces about the past-happier times in the four lines ending in "had a happy inner song"-peace, love, pleasure- "with others sharing a past" [when he] escaped [despair] so well so long." In the last two lines the "simple tune [a simple happy life is]/now gone."

For Silence [no date]
The children are asleep
a fire[']s crack is all I hear
On this night so deep and still.
I think about our quiet life
and wonder why beneath my
breast all thoughts lie dead.
Where is this match I seek.
I speak all day and much
at night but my dreams of
you all lie unsaid.
Why so mute with tender phrases
-pure love-happiness-content-and more
when I feel the pleasure of there [their] glow.
Could they if told lead to a fatal
blow-no
But none will flow because of
of some tight unseen band

which is about my chest. This
thing that I cannot explain.
I hope this paradox is mine
alone and locks on other[']s breasts
are burned away as words
unfold for lovers to behold.

This poem creates an atmosphere of quiet. His "children are asleep." He only hears "a fire's crack"-in the fireplace-reminiscent of his buried ardor. Otherwise, the night is "deep and still" and he thinks about his and his wife's quiet life [incommunicado]. This leads him to question why his thoughts of her "lie dead"-are not spoken. He asks himself "where is this match I seek?" He is aware that he "speaks all day and much/at night but my [his] dreams of you [her] all lie unsaid." He wants a connection back. Is the match he seeks also in reference to his intention of igniting a fire with a match? And is the match also the spark of intimacy between himself and his mate which seems to have gone dormant?

In lines eleven through nineteen he asks himself what prevents him from making his feelings known-"Why so mute with tender phrases/-pure love-happiness-content-and more/when I feel the pleasure of there [their] glow." His hidden pleasure creates a glow-as if from the fire's embers-but is left unspoken. Next, he questions whether or not his disclosure would be received well or not-"Could they if told lead to a fatal/ blow?" He answers "No". However, he really isn't so sure how his declarations might be received, for he keeps his thoughts to himself. He describes his trepidation as follows-"But none [no words] will flow because / of some tight unseen band/which is about my chest." This tight

Love Poems and Obsession

band is a manifestation of his anxious uncertainty-which keeps him silent. His paradox is his wanting to speak and yet unable for fear of a rebuff.

In the final four lines he writes-"I hope this paradox is mine/ alone and locks on other[']s/ breasts/are burned away as words/ unfold for lovers to behold". I think he speaks here of all lovers everywhere being able to have what he hopes for-honest and intimate communication. Again, he uses the fire simile-"...locks on other ['] s breasts [hearts]/ are burned away..."-and the lock is broken. Fire is a catalyst for purification. Fire is ardor, emotional warmth, passion, enthusiasm, and zeal (#9, pg. 211, American Century Dictionary). He hopes his lover will not be like him-with a lock of insecurity about his breast-but able to freely speak her heart and mind-which would unlock his own heart.

Today [no date]
today
I thought of you alone getting dinner ready for our coming home
today
On arrival not much was said but cherishment was our poem
Then a peaceful meal later did portend
How a regular evening was going to end
In quiet love that does not shout
But covers us like a warm mantle about
For the laughter, cries, taunts and all
are always for a spirit pleasurable to recall.
Such simple things
no I say
God nothing better ever brings.

I wonder about this poem that follows the last. I wonder about a double meaning in this poem. Dad starts out with two manifestations of his day-"Today" he thinks of her "...alone getting dinner ready for our coming home"-him and us kids. Then, "Today/On arrival not much was said but cherishment was our poem." Since nothing was said, how does he know that they shared "cherishment"? (#10, pg. 251 –"to hold dear, value highly...to treat tenderly: foster; nurture; to hold in mind"). In the next line he says that "...a peaceful meal did portend (#11, pg. 1138-an omen, warning, or less frequently, a presage (#12, pg. 1152-to predict) how a regular evening was going to end." The usual meaning for portend is an omen or warning, and less common, a presage or prediction, so there may be a few possibilities for the meaning of "portend" in this context. Then he tells us the evening ended in "quiet love that does not shout/But covers us like a warm mantle about". Did they share intimate moments under the covers? The word mantle (#13, pg. 894) may suggest protection (a cover) or something that is concealed (hidden)-their lovemaking or was it contempt, apathy? Or is it what he hoped for- intimate moments under a cloud of blankets?

In the next two lines he cites "laughter, cries, [even] taunts and all/are always of a spirit to recall. Really? What about taunts?-(#14, pg. 1493), meaning reproach, scornful or jeering remarks. Maybe I'm influenced by previous poems that describe his hesitancy (or even inability) to reveal his feeling to her. He has also described her as if he doesn't really know what she's thinking or feeling. Although she had a "quiet affect" and that "not much was said" upon his arrival home, might that suggest indifference, even anger on her part? But he reads this as their shared cherishment. How so? But then, maybe he really felt some sort of quiet connection with her that went both ways and wrote this poem to celebrate it. Maybe he was just trying to be hopeful. I do know that there was a long period of time in their marriage when there was friction.

Embraced [no date]
I sat and half aloud tried long to compose.
A short verse to tell you how I adore thee,
And though this feeling ran from my
heart along with the blood to permiate [permeate],
a portion, to each part.
Dumbfounded, as though we sat face to face,
no further words than these could this
pen trace other than to say; I truly live
in adoration for you embraced.
Bob

This poem describes (in lines one through 5) his thinking "half aloud" how to go about expressing his deepest feelings for his beloved- "A short verse". He was able to utter his thoughts half aloud while not in her physical presence. His feelings traveled from his heart's blood to permeate this feeling to each part of his being. In the last four lines, he describes feeling "dumbfounded" as though they were "face to face"-the implication here is that the imagined physical intimate presence of her is intimidating and makes him mute. The thought even makes it difficult for him to pen his feelings-"No further words than these could this/pen trace…" but he is able to say [write] the one phrase that gives him a voice with his pen-"I truly live in adoration for you embraced". He doesn't say he lives in adoration of her, but for her-He gives his adoration as a gift for her and ends this sentence with the word "embraced" (#15, pg. 473). The word embraced has several meanings that may all apply-To clasp…as an expression of affection or desire/ to accept readily/ to encircle, surround, enclose/ and also to set on fire, incite, instigate. All may have been in his mind in writing this phrase. Dad was a big proponent of his dictionary. He often read through pages at a time to improve his vocabulary and/or to find just the right word to help him express himself as carefully as possible.

Jean-How I Feel [May 21, 1966]
Like Dylan [Thomas] I must say I love you
with every pore it sounds so sweet to me
like poetry the ever trite I love you.
I feel your presence next to me with drink
or sober always the same your soul &
body part of me our spirits together
as only we can know. A thought or
place in our hearts entwined
a common bond no other human can
share it[']s ours how fine how unique.
Our spirits know what I seek in the
words above in depth of field
In solitude you know what I feel for
we feel alike confident of love like
few alive. What a gift. What a life-
What a love. Cherish with ever increasing
feeling each year in its passing. Only
better because it was spent together

in bond of mutual love
I sit tonight with alcohol as an
an ally to set free a tongue so
tied when in front [of you] I can't say
what I feel so deep so fundamental
inside. Why not say over and
over again what in my heart
sits–Why not–When sober or
in regular course–I don't know
it [']s never released & few times
even with drink . I can't
explain this lack of voice
that pen allowes [allows] to expres [express]
but not the voice. I feel
we play captive to our past
and though we try few
true feelings drive past our
artificial fringe to find
a place expressed
so if done even clumsily at
best my heart and
soul have been undressed.
To you my love I only feel my
heart and soul have been undressed.
I want you to know If you
said but a wish, to me[-]If
I could grant it [-] it would be.
I speak not of earthly wants

but of things I know are
more precious to you and
me. Like just a pat [,] a
caress or more in jest or
for more serious score. But
always with love and
and scope more broad than
simple quest of emotion. For
our sitelement [statement?] [settlement?] [sentiment?]
is greater than
a brief emotional encounter
for it lasts in spirit more
Than in flesh. So farewell
tonight True love and may
we see future union of soul
and flesh as we have in past
encounters- I hope your satisfaction
lies with mine so all will [be?]
as well with you as it has
been with me.
[with] Love
It reads well with proper intent so
feel you should get the
feeling that I meant.

This is the first poem in the collection that is dated-May 21, 1966. The date was written in by Mom. Her cursive was quite different than Dad's. I was fifteen at the time, and had been aware of both of my parent's struggles-Dad's more apparent. Events preceded this difficult time-Dad's anguish about a medical mishap, his finding solace of some sort in another woman or two, Mom's distress over Dad's emotional state and her suspicions about his infidelity. I had only clues and hints at the time about the reasons for the upheaval in our home-all the fun came to a screeching halt. Dad wept for hours in his bed at night, was silent, sometimes rage-full in the day. Sometimes there were angry words and shouting between them at the dinner table-but back to the poem.

This poem spans four full pages. Its cursive is more loose and words and phrases more rambling than usual. There were also some words I had to guess at. His mention of drink throughout the poem may explain this style of writing in this piece. The theme of the poem is that of its title-how he feels about her and their relationship. This is expressed in the first page and throughout the rest of the poem.

In the first page of this four page poem Dad will wax poetic with ever increasing romantic intensity. He likens himself to the poet Dylan Thomas [the Welch poet, born October 27th, 1914 and died November 9th, 1953]-"Like Dylan I must say I love you/ with every pore [of my being] it sounds so sweet to me/ like poetry the ever trite I love you." There is hardly room for him to take a breath if he was to speak this page rather than pen it, his thoughts come so fast and furious, running one into the other, with the intensity of exuberant emotion. There seems he has a confidence that they share this passion-"...our spirits together as only we can know", "...our hearts entwined", "...we feel alike confident of love like few alive", "What a gift. What a life-What a love".

The remaining pages may just as well been written at a different time altogether and/or in a different frame of mind. However, I think he did write this poem in one sitting. It's just that the first page was written with his optimism but the tone changes in the remaining pages as doubt and insecurity-his very different frame of mind-takes over. The theme of his difficulty speaking freely to his beloved is addressed here again. Again, on page two, he confesses that it is much easier for him to pen his feelings rather than telling her how he feels. The result is less likely to bring on a rebuff or indifference on her part. So, here he is on his second page-…"with alcohol as an ally to set free the tongue so tied when [you are] in front [of me] I can't say what I feel so deep so fundamental inside [me]". Near the end of the second page he offers a guess at his fear of opening up to her-"I fear/ we play captive to our past/ and though we try/ few true feelings drive past our artificial fringe…" The fringe (#16, pg.581) is a type of border-keeping things out-and is artificial (#17, pg. 84) because the silence is unnatural or affected. Each of their pasts instill insecurity and vulnerability that make them mute-maybe Mom's family dynamic, as she grew up, and Dad's immigrant background. They are captive to their past personal difficulties, insecurities, betrayals, etc. But he is able to push past his barrier with his pen and he hopes both of them will find some sort of voice for the other.

On page three there is another emotional shift. He starts out- "So if done even clumsily at best my heart and soul have been undressed./To you my love I only feel my heart and soul have been undressed". He has made himself vulnerable to her with his poem, and only her. Again, the focus changes in the last half of this page

(3). Now he speaks of doing anything possible to strengthen their union–"I want you to know If you/said but a wish, to me [,] If/I could grant it [,] it would be." But this would not be some trifle request–"... not of earthy wants/but of things I know are/more precious to you and me. Like just a pat [,] a /caress or more in jest or/for more serious score".

On page four, he elaborates–"[but even a]... scope more broad than simple quest of emotion." What he speaks of is something that "...lasts in spirit more than in flesh." Next, he hopes for a bright future–"[with a]...future union of soul and flesh as we have in past encounters..." In the last four lines of the poem before he signs off with Love, he hopes her feelings will match his, but it seems to me he's not sure. His postscript is a rhyme–"It reads well with proper intent so/ feel you should get the/ feeling that I meant." He hopes she understands his intent, but again, seems unsure of what she hopes for.

Alone [July, 1967]

Often if alone my thoughts drift

to you

Sweet pleasure often melancholy

binds me.

Alone silent joy feeds my spirit

and I pass an hour rich for that

one brief moment.

This date, again, was in Mom's hand and the next poem shares a page with Alone. Both seem to have been written in tandem. By this time, Mom had given birth on June 5th, 1967 to their fourth and last child, Nora. This child was planned and, in fact, Mom suffered a miscarriage before Nora was conceived. Dad's sister, Jean, and their cousin from Slovenija, Yanko, were visiting during the time Dad wrote these two poems. Dad seemed out of sorts during his relative's visit-irritable I'll have to say-and maybe also preoccupied as "Alone" suggests. Again, he uses the word "drifts". It shows up again and again in his poems. In this one's first line-"Often if alone my thoughts drift/to you"-he elaborates about how these drifting thoughts affect him-[with] "Sweet pleasure [but also] often melancholy/ [that] binds me." He is obligated to her through both love and duty, and on some level even paralyzed by the feelings his beloved evokes in him. In the last three lines he relishes his private time, in thoughts of her-"Alone silent joy feeds my spirit/and I pass an hour rich for that/ one brief moment." In the big scheme of things- then what? Maybe his preoccupation with her left him bereft of energy for his guests and maybe there were other demons he was also preoccupied with.

Threads [July, 1967]
Threads of time together entwine
Each good moment adding another
The cord if death should part us
Unraveled through space
will still
join your heart and mine.

This twin poem to Alone seems to go a step further than the first. In Alone, the focus was on his daydreaming [how it was an enriching experience, albeit melancholic at the same time] and how all other stimuli should be ignored. The poem Threads seems mystical by comparison. It suggests timelessness. Dad starts out, however, speaking of time-"threads of time" are woven together-"entwined" into the whole. So "Each good moment" is a thread woven into the fabric. In the third line the threads have formed an umbilical cord. He goes on to say that even if death should part them and "the cord ...unraveled through space", it "will still/ join your heart and mine" because time will no longer be a factor. Eternity will maintain their bond.

In the poem Alone there is focus on temporal time and its fleeting quality, ever changing. The poem Threads distinguishes itself from its partner-transforming its "threads of time to an unraveling cord, still intact in the mysterious timelessness of eternity.

The Simple Things [January, 1968]
The simple things are best of all
like a quiet day alone with you.
When only words of kindness pass
like they very often do.

A simple poem named "The Simple Things". Mom, again, writes in the date. I'm thankful for these bits of information. It helps me add context to each poem she dates, for then I can interject myself and my siblings into the time frame she provides. Here Dad simply states that such simple moments that he describes here are often the most significant in any relationship. The day is quiet, they are alone together, and their conversation is made up of "words of kindness." He adds that these times when kind words are shared is the norm for them. As in other of his poems, his relationship with his wife (a sense of creating a world apart, from all else, for the two of them) is his focus.

Drifts [February 10, 1968]
Un [-] matters time or doing my mind

drifts – to you.
Encountering form and face.
Evenescent [Evanescent] joy-passed.
Drifting [,] doing.

Here is another simple poem written not long after the previous one-"The Simple Things". The tone of "Drifts" is also similar to the last. He is quiet, calm, and meditative. He starts out with "Un-matters time"-or, more simply, time doesn't matter when speaking of matters of the soul. First, he is telling her that time spent on his daydreams matters, but what doesn't matter [un-matters] is time itself. Here, he is "doing [his] mind drifts- to [her]"- in this case, his mind drifts to daydreams of her- "encountering [both her] form and face" which brings on "evanescent [# 18, pg.502-tending to fade from sight; vanishing; ephemeral] [#19, pg. 487, ephemeral-short-lived; transitory] joy" which then "passed" because this evanescent joy of his is short-lived and transitory as human mental images all tend to be. After images of her fade, he goes back to "Drifting [,] doing" which seems less precise and more free-flowing. The last line-"Drifting - Doing" seems to connote an eternal quality-leading back to the reference in the first line-"Un-matters time." This pleasant way to pass his time continues on wherever it is that his mind will take him and maybe his consciousness will even transcend his eventual death.

40 [April 6, 1968]
Long days
Long duties
More demand more

Deem more
Back-Brain-Body
Beat
Retire - Refreshed
Repeat-Repeat-Repeat
Yet
Nearly Over

In April of 1968 all four of us kids were still living at home. Mom had a nearly year old Nora to look after and then there was Doug, an energetic eleven year old boy, and Sandy and me-fifteen and seventeen-respectively. Mom was a few months from her fortieth birthday, as the title indicates. It seems, according to Dad's observations presented in this poem, that it was all too much for her. The forth line-"Deem more" suggests that Dad is able to (#20, pg. 383, deem-to think, believe, judge) the situation that presented itself even more astutely-'Back-Brain-Body/Beat". Then the day will end-"Retire-Refreshed"-but the drudgery-"Repeat-Repeat-Repeat" continues for her (or them) day after day. Finally, he writes-"Yet/Nearly Over". Is he looking ahead to a repose [#21, pg. 1235, rest from work, travel, etc.; calm, tranquility, peace; to rest in a grave]? Is he alluding to the finite aspect of a human's life?-A more permanent rest from worldly toil-Death?-which may offer a final peace and eternal bliss together.

Is he looking to the future when they will be left alone? Mom was a serious, often humorless person, especially when faced with responsibility. I'm unsure which of them was more motivated to have their fourth child when Dad was already forty and Mom was thirty eight. It did happen and this isn't the only poem that speaks to Dad's observation that Mom may not have been up to the task to handle an infant and three other growing children. However, we did all leave, one at a time, and they were left with maybe what was necessary for them to carry on together in a more satisfactory relationship.

Hate to See [no date]
Hate to see the baby cry
And you too
I love you–I love you
What more can I do.

There isn't a date to this short four line poem but it fits in with the previous one. Dad "Hate[s] to see the baby cry/ and you too". He tells her in the poem [twice] that he loves her and asks without a question mark at the end–"What more can I do." What I'm unsure about is whether or not he helped Mom with Nora's care during what he perceived as difficult times for Nora's mother [Mom]. I do know that he always spent time with the first three of us, including all forms of childcare when it wasn't really in fashion to do so in the 1950's and '60's. I'm not sure about diaper changing though. I do think that Mom struggled with motherhood long before Nora came along.

Tired [no date]
Much Toil
No help True
Children fun
Till ['til] about two [o'clock]
On & On
Hours take a tole [toll]

Wearyness [Weariness] hits
Yet more to go
Holidays too few
Then
Turmoiled years
are through
Only love left
Will it do.

This poem has a similar topic as the last two. Again, there is no date. It seems a twin poem to "Hate to See". They are placed on the same page of the poetry album which had a large "J" on its cover. The "J" stands for Mom's middle name-Jean. No one ever called Mom by her first given name-Frances-at least, not that I'm aware of. This poem is also reminiscent of "40". Dad must have been an observer of Mom's shutting down during this period of their lives. Was adding another child at Mom's age something Dad promoted? Or was the decision a mutual one?

In the first four lines Dad describes "Much Toil/No help True [Is the "True" added because Dad is agreeing with Mom's opinion that she bears the childcare responsibility?]-/children fun/ Till ['til] about two"-[in the afternoon?] The next four lines continue to describe [maybe] both of their struggles-"On & On/ Hours take a tole [toll] / Wearyness [Weariness] hits/Yet more to go." Then he writes that "Holidays [are] too few"-Before the new baby they had come to enjoy very frequent adventures of their own. This was a time that I found myself in charge of the household and my siblings, and now this would include my baby sister, in what seemed to me, at least, to remain very frequent occurrences.

I suspect that Dad's focus on Mom's perceived struggles, after Nora came along, had more to do with her long history of general discontent with domestic life than with the addition of a new baby. My own awareness of my mother's domestic discontent was never voiced by me, but upon reflection, I think I was aware and that it instilled in me a fear early on that I might find myself in the same predicament if I wasn't careful. This worry didn't, however, prevent me from following in her footsteps. I guess her being a role model for me, good or bad, was a greater incentive than to rebel against it-at least for a while. I did tend to model my parenting style more after my father than my mother, though. He seemed more fun and more engaged in his parental role than Mom. Or maybe I just took more after Dad in disposition, making him seem more interesting to me.

There is a shift in the last five lines of this poem. After stating all the problems in the first nine lines, he changes course with the one line word "then"-[what happens next?]-"Turmoiled years/are through"-He projects himself and Mom into the future when they are alone. He then asks the question that when "only love is left/ Will it do." There is no question mark as he often leaves them off what could be a question. This leaves more room for speculation. "Will it do" could be heard or interpreted as-["I will it to"-"I" added and "do" easily changed into "to"] or the question-If only our love is left without interference, will it suffice [be enough]?

Had a coctail [cocktail] [September 1969]
Had a coctail [cocktail]
Thought of you.
During [Driving or Dining]

You drifted
Through
Listened to
a lecture
interspersed
by you.
Keep drifting
Back [to you-crossed out]
Nothing else
I want to do.
You [cross out] [made or make]
me happy
Through &
Through

This poem stands alone on the page. I was just leaving home for my first year of college. Mom was the one who would date this poem. He writes in the first two lines-"Had a coctail [cocktail]/Thought of you." The next three lines either tell that "During [Driving or Dining]/ you drifted /Through [my mind]" Then later on, he "Listened to/a lecture [I suspect at a medical conference] /interspersed by [thoughts of] you." She interrupted his focus, or squelched his boredom? As the lecture continues he will "Keep drifting/back/ [he crosses out the words to you] [There is] Nothing else/I want to do." He remains preoccupied with thoughts of her. In the last four lines-"You [cross out] made [or make]/me happy/ through and through"-Dad wants to convey the pleasure he conjures up with his daydreams of her. The first cross out appears to be the word "can", and the word "make" seems to have been changed to "made". The sentiment "you can make/me happy" is very different from "you made me happy", for the second puts her making him happy in the past tense as opposed to the first rendering which suggests that, if she wants, she is able to make him happy. Still, he hopes to convey the pleasure he conjures up with his daydreams of her. As mentioned, he also crossed out the words "to you" in line 10 of the poem. Why did he do this? Does his daydreaming lead him away from thoughts of her and then to thoughts of his own doubt about her feelings for him?

This is the first of many in the album that focuses on his thoughts, feelings and loneliness while they are separated from each other, whether it be her physical or emotional absence. The poem was written on a restaurant place mat, one of many poems written on various forms for his writing-suggesting that, while he wrote, there was at least his physical absence from her.

We drift together [September, 1969]
We drift together
Separate shells
Touching at will
and random
Time passed paths
Parallel – converge
Then merged
continue onward,
Blessed with
purpose and need.

This poem examines coincidence, fate, and intent in coupling. It starts out-"We drift together/Separate shells"-indicative of romantic chance meetings. In their case, the first was while Mom was fourteen, Dad sixteen, in the halls of their high school. Their acquaintance was fleeting. He asked to see her report card in the school's hallway. She was shy but showed him anyway. He often brought up this chance meeting and exclaiming that he was impressed with the card. His next two lines-"Touching at will/and random" suggests there were contrived bouts of mingling-"touching at will" but also unplanned, chance meetings-"and random". One of these random meetings was after WWII. Dad had resumed his college studies and Mom was working as a soda fountain jerk on the Elmhurst College Campus-"Time passed paths/parallel-converge/Then merged"-this meeting was significant and led to a torrid courtship and marriage. Then Dad writes-"continue onward/Blessed with/purpose and need." It's all a matter of chance or fate, but in the end there is intent, commitment, and necessity.

When Dad uses the words "Separate shells" in the second line, the description seems to suggest that when separate, they are, in essence, empty. When they "… merged/ [then] continue[d] onward", they are no longer empty shells, but instead, whole and "Blessed with/purpose and need."

Fasten for a moment [October, 1970]
Fasten for a moment your
eyes to mine.
Dream of golden grapes
Ripened on a vine.
Oh fastening sweeter
than their wine.
Draws back-silent bliss
sublime.

In this poem Dad asks Mom to "Fasten for a moment your eyes to mine." He always was fascinated, in fact, in love with her eyes. The next two lines allude to the hypnotic power of their eye contact-how they can both "Dream of golden grapes ripened on a vine."-Just as their love ripens with their mutual gaze, the poem tells us that their eyes that "fasten" on each other are like the golden vine-ripened grapes fastened on the vine. Then, in the fifth and sixth lines, he tells the reader that their gaze, just as the grapes on the vine, is even sweeter than the grape's wine.

Dad connects the words "fasten" in line one and "fastening" in line five to accentuate the similarity he sees between their mutual gaze and the grapes fastened on the vine-a steadfast connection. He creates a simile between eyes and grapes. In the last two lines, Dad "Draws back" [takes it all in and relishes in their mutual gaze]- "silent bliss/sublime". No words are necessary for this intimate silent communication, which leads to his sublime and blissful state. Sublime's meaning is (# 22, pg. 1452- inspiring awe or admiration through grandeur, beauty, etc; Also [poetic], elated, joyful). Bliss is (#23, pg. 157-rapture; ecstasy).

Dreams [February 14, 1971]

Dreams

Exist – Drift

about – float

freely. Flit

through–mostly

of you.

Moments of

pleasure. Instant

warmth–with

residual glow

Love Poems and Obsession

don [']t want to
let it go-
Ephemeral-
concept grows.

This Valentine's Day poem is about daydreams-a very familiar topic of Dad's. In the first six lines he says that "Dreams Exist" and seem to have a life of their own. They "Drift/about - float/ freely" [and] "Flit/through [his mind]-mostly/of you" [her]. Float is (#24, pg. 555, to drift gently; move without effort). Flit is (#25, pg. 555, passing lightly and rapidly ...through the mind). The poem shifts focus in the seventh through the fourteenth lines. His thoughts become more focused. They travel to "moments of pleasure" which lead to "instant warmth-with residual glow"-He seems here to be referring to sexual union and afterglow. "The warmth", the "residual glow", conjure up a vision of dying embers in a fire place. Mom and Dad often sat next to the fireplace in the family room with a fire going. He doesn't "want to let it go", for he fears his thoughts and feelings are "Ephemeral (#26, pg. 487, transitory). But then-the "concept grows". The word concept-(#27, pg. 302, from the word conceive-is to imagine, apprehend, to express or represent in words) as he does in this poem. And by doing so, he preserves his dreams, his memories, his feelings on paper. And the "concept grows"-it thrives and becomes more significant, maybe even everlasting. This poem was written on a piece of a paper restaurant place mat. He always used whatever was available wherever he found himself to pen and save his experience.

Thanks- [2-16-71]
Thanks-

It is as warm
As your love but
Not nearly as
Beautiful
Sorry about the salad
The tender care was
obvious

Dad dated this poem. It comes two days past the previous one. He thanks Mom for some unknown kindness-a gift, a card? He says- "It is as warm/as your love but/not nearly as/beautiful" He is telling her that whatever she gave him-a scarf, gloves, coat, sentimental card [something warm]-is appreciated. But the gift can't compare to her love for him which he labels as "beautiful". Then there is the line drawn on the same sheet of paper to divide this poem from the next. I believe they were written in tandem or maybe within a day or two-his cursive is a little different between the two, though, and the emotional flavor is also different. Take a look.

I suspect Dad said something stupidly insensitive and/or insulting to require his apology-"Sorry about the salad." Dad liked vinegar and oil salads, heavy on the vinegar, he grew up on. Sometimes he'd add the inside of a hot baked potato-the result was a hearty wilted side dish-this, a Slovenian/Italian influence from his mother. Mom grew up without salads at all, but during my growing up years we had the V & O style for every evening meal anyway. I suspect she tried something different for a change and suffered a rebuff. Dad tries to make up for it with his apology-"the tender care was/obvious." I especially liked his stick drawing figures on the bottom of the page-She flees and he follows in her direction with his pleas for her forgiveness.

Love Poems and Obsession

Alone Reflecting [9-15-72]
Alone reflecting
What would I say
If we were alone
some day.
No intruders
just ourselves
on a short
grand holiday
Would we just past the time
Of day
Nothing ['] s not
what we would say
No but talk of
Dew, flowers,
love and of
running barefoot
too
And = again I'd
Declare my
Love to
You.
Reflecting Ryan's
9-15-72
[with] Kssah
1:30

Here again is a divided page poem but seems more integrated than the last-Thanks & Sorry. Dad used two different sheets of small notebook paper and placed one below the other but there is only the one title for both sections-Alone reflecting. The two sections have different writing styles. In the first, the cursive is irregular. Some words are written in a heavier hand than others. There is subtle evidence of erased and rewritten words. His cursive is also rather irregular. The second section is a continuation of the first in subject matter. It elaborates on and answers the question posed in the first-"What would I say". It also exhibits a steadier hand, a more regular cursive style, no evidence of cross-outs or rewrites. This leads me to believe that they were written with some lapse of time in between.

In the first section Dad tells his spouse, audience, or himself, that he is "Alone reflecting." He tries to imagine what he would say to her if they were alone together. The next word "someday" suggests that this state is rare-"Alone reflecting/what would I say/ If we were alone/someday." There seems to be little opportunity for them to have uninterrupted intimate conversation because there are still "intruders" in the home-their kids.

Next, Dad daydreams of the future when there is opportunity- "just ourselves/on a short/grand holiday." He asks-"Would we just/ pass the time/of day" [in silence?] He answers his own question- "Nothing ['] s not/what we would say"-because there would be opportunity for intimacy and uninterrupted conversation-he hopes.

In the second section, Dad elaborates on how things would be. He reiterates with a "No"-to his question in the first section and then elaborates-"…but [they would] talk of/dew, flowers,/love and of/running barefoot/too"-creating a virtual Garden of Eden. In this garden, he'd find his voice-"And again I'd/declare my/love to

Love Poems and Obsession

you/Reflecting" He ends with the same word found in the title and first line of the poem-"reflecting" which brings him to an awareness that, at least for now, his imaginings are only that. He signs off-"Ryan's" [one of their favorite haunts in Portland, Oregon], the date-"9-15-72", [with kisses or -"Kssah"?]-Is he signing off with kisses or is Kssah initials of a staffer or patron at Ryan's? This time-"1:30"-Is it A.M. or P.M.? He must be alone and away from home.

Mental Imagery [no date]
Sit and philosophically examine
The world at present and in rest.
Reflect on now and on the past.
Where do [these] pleasures lie [?]
Mainly un [-] mental,
Sadly in physical repast.
So thank you now because my
Mental pleasure is aglow.
Contrasted to less than one man per
Millennium touching a [-] physical sublimily [sublimity]
A state so familiar to me
My dreams are ten times ten then
a touch and
The aftermath times ten again.
And yet the state of our affair
Lies at one for me on a scale of
Ten relative to Infinity.
Kerk [19]72

In this poem Dad describes contemplation of the world. He looks at things "at present and in rest."-That is, not in motion. He reflects "on now [rest] and [also] on the past. He asks himself-"Where do pleasures lie [?]" He answers "mainly un [-] mental," [but rather with sensuality]. Then he adds that these pleasures are "sadly in physical repast." Repast is (#28, pg.1233-food and drink; [or more broadly] sustenance of life). In the seventh line he thanks his lover and wife because she is responsible for his mental pleasure being "aglow" [in emotion]. He then compares himself to almost all other men "per millennium"- [of a thousand years] able to touch "a-physical" [non-physical] "sublimily [sublimity]. The definition of sublime is (#29, pg. 1452; 2. inspiring awe or admiration; 3. [Poetic], elated; joyful.) Dad says this sublimity is "a state so familiar to [him]." He reaches it often because of her-his dreams [of her] are "ten times ten."-compared to others' pleasure. Then "a touch and/the aftermath [of the touch is] ten times ten again." Ten times ten and then ten times ten again equals a millennium. Their love, he feels, is that rare and powerful. "And yet" in spite of this millennium, he says that this state of their affair lies only "at one" for him, compared to a scale of ten in relation to the scope and possibilities of his emotion and devotion that spans infinity. The definition of infinity is (#30, pg. 748, 2. endless or unlimited space, time, distance, quality, etc.). He signs this poem Kerk-his nickname, with the date 1972. He crosses out one attempt at a drawing of a bird and replaces it with another-It's beak with an x (mathematical times sign) next to it-pointing at the word infinity. My feeling is that the bird signifies flight to eternity. I also want to add that, in this poem and in others, I see the influence of Dad's scientific-math, physics, chemistry, etc. learning that he melds with his spirituality.

Erased [7-19-73]
Ran north along the ocean for a mile or so
Found a lonely segment of beach
Houses high no ladders led below
There alone before an incomming [incoming] tide
I traced a message dedicated to
The birthday of my love.
Perchance
It happened to be slightly late
Mind dwells on the message none will see
Except those departed and me
Like a mind etched from birth to rest
The incomming [incoming] Tide will soon erase
every trace
before she passes that perfect place.
FRK 7-19-73

This poem was written during a stay at our family beach spot. Mom and Dad often went there on their own though. Dad tells of a run on the beach he took the day before-Mom's birthday. First, he "Ran north along the ocean for a mile or so", then "found a lonely segment of beach/ houses high no ladders led below [to the shore]"-He's all by himself, entirely alone, on this stretch of beach-so it is unlikely he will encounter any other soul while on his trek. Then, "there alone before an incoming tide [he] traced a message dedicated to the birthday of [his] love." With the one word line-"Perchance" the focus of the poem shifts and Dad adds "It happened to be slightly late/mind dwells on the message none will see/except those departed and me." I think this speaks to his inability to communicate with his beloved, as seen in numerous of his poems, but this time, only he and those departed will see his message. His audience also isn't privy to the message in the sand, only he and souls departed from this earth. There is another shift in the last four lines. He likens his message to "a mind from birth to rest [that] the incoming tide will soon erase/every trace." Maybe he speaks here of his insignificance. Maybe he speaks of the kindred aloneness of us all. And maybe, on a more personal level, he speaks to his pervasive inability to reach his wife on an intimate, emotional level, for his message written at "that perfect place" will never be seen by her. The place is perfect because if she had read it, he would have expressed his sentiment to her successfully. It is perfect too because the message was written in a private, solitary and beautiful spot in nature, reminiscent of the divine. But she will eventually pass that perfect place-it's just that it will be too late.

There is also another theme that seems to pervade this poem. It, too, has been seen before in his other poems. Dad hints at human annihilation at death-"Like a mind etched from birth to rest/the incomming [incoming] Tide [capitalized-the cycle of life-the ebb and flow?] will soon erase/every trace" [of his message]. However, he has also alluded to some form of consciousness after death in other of his poems and, in this particular one, he also wrote that "those departed" were all that shared his secret message with him.

Yet Alive [K-11-73]
Complicated thIng you make my
Heart sing
Yet your cut subtle nuance drops
my affect to nothing.

Un [-] perfect as I am - I am
my bag good or sad.
Near 50 now
the trend is set – set hard
Natural thing – Unnatural way
Exposed to heat will
Steel's temper hold
Or will
the sear effect collapse
leaving alone a deserted
life [-] time of my own.
Sadly will I say
I died tomorrow – today.
Happily K – 11-73

It seems to me that Dad expresses hurt feelings in this poem, and maybe also anger, confusion, and irritation too. In the first two lines he calls Mom a "complicated thing" [who] makes his "heart sing". In spite of her perplexing, but also pleasing him, he follows with an accusation–"your cut subtle nuance drops/ my affect to nothing." Cut is (#31, pg. 364, 12. an act, remark, etc. that hurts one's feelings) similar to cutting (#32, pg. 365, adj. 3. wounding the feelings; sarcastic). The word subtle is (#33, pg. 1455, 4. crafty; artful; wily; designing. 7. acting in an insidious way). Nuance is (#34, pg. 1006, a slight or delicate variation in tone, color, meaning, etc.; shade of difference). I add these definitions to emphasize how the combination of these three words–"cut subtle nuance" describes her influence over him–a loss of his integrity (#35, pg. 759, 1. the quality or state of being complete; unbroken;...) of being and his consequential descent into perdition-(#36, pg. 1085, 1. complete and irreparable loss; ruin). The result of her "cut subtle nuance" is described in the entire two lines-"Yet your cut subtle nuance drops/my affect to nothing." This observation of her malice and its dire effect on him couldn't be more damaging. It speaks to his extinction, annihilation. How could one be hurt more by another?

In the fifth line Dad attempts to respond to the wound she inflicts on him-"Imperfect as I am-I am/My bag good or sad." His bag is all that he is made of and instead of describing his bag as the conventional phrase-"good or bad" (although this phrase applies too), he writes "good or sad"-I believe, to emphasize his emotional state as compared to "bad"-a character flaw that he seems to accept; instead, "sad" returns the reader's focus to the hurt he feels.

In the seventh line the tone changes slightly. He turns to himself and starts out-"Near 50 now"-(he was 47 and Mom was 45) - "The trend is set-set hard/Natural thing-[My] Unnatural way [compared to her natural way]. A few definitions of natural are (#37, pg. 977, 1. "arising from nature; 4. a)...wild, uncultivated; b) unenlightened, primitive). Compare to definitions of unnatural-(#38, pg. 1594, 3. characterized by a lack of emotions, attitudes, or behavior regarded as natural, normal, or right.). So here we have their basic differences. He compares his unnatural way to steel-[My] "Unnatural way/ [if] Exposed to heat will/steel's temper hold" [?]-If steel is tempered, it is- (#39, pg. 1499, 1. To make suitable, desirable by... mingling with something else; reduce intensity...moderate...;mollify: as, temper your criticism with reason; 2. to bring to proper texture, consistency, hardness, etc. by mixing with something or treating in some way: ...steel...is tempered by heating and sudden cooling;). The next question he asks is-"Or will/the sear [heating] effect collapse [?] Will trying to change himself end in his destruction ["collapse"]? If so, the result will be "leaving ... [only] a deserted lifetime of ...[his] own"-annihilation along with the loss of her. Then, Dad writes-"Sadly will I say/I died tomorrow – today." I think, here, he anticipates and predicts his emotional death if he loses himself and/or her. So he sadly says today that he will die tomorrow. There may also be some effort on his part to warp the concept of time, which is consistent with his bent towards timelessness in his poetry-today, tomorrow-what's the difference? Below the poem he adds the word-"Happily." I wonder if he added it to suggest that despite the outcome-his emotional death and/or his losing her-it was still all worth it. The title of this poem is also telling-"Yet Alive" for it suggests the paradox of the poem's inconsistencies and disputes the end, his death, which makes room for hope-even if it's only his dying "Happily".

Dust.? [no date]
Stardust formed cosmos
Born of your special
sellar [stellar] [solar] dust.
In celestial reaction
has captured my form
and vast as it may be
The remaining nebulae
Mean much less
to me

Cheryl Krkoč

Dad often speaks of universal concepts-romance, magic, or ethereality. His scientific schooling-mathematics, physics, chemistry, biology influenced his belief system. So, maybe, did his Catholic upbringing and Old World influence from his immigrant parents, other relatives and enclave of such in the Chicago area.

This poem is full of cosmic words and phrases. Cosmic dust is (#40, pg. 333, small particles, probably meteoric fragments, falling from interstellar space to earth. Cosmos is (#41, pg. 334, n. [Mod. Latin, Greek- kosmos; universe, world, order, harmony]. 1. the universe considered as a harmonious and orderly system: opposed to chaos). Stellar is (#42, pg. 1428, 1. of the stars, stardust). Chaos is (#43, pg. 245, 1. the disorder of formless matter and infinite space, supposed to have existed before the ordered universe). The title "Dust" with a question mark-dust is mysterious, the element of all? He goes on to say that stardust is the elemental building block of the cosmos.

In the second and third lines-"born of your special sellar [stellar] dust" suggests that the cosmos was born [evolved] from his lover's "special stellar dust"-implying that she is the causal property of the universal-his universe. He writes the word "sellar' rather than "stellar". I suspect he meant stellar, meaning stardust, but the word "sellar" may also have been a combination of the words "solar" and "stellar". Solar is (#44, pg. 1386, 1. of or having to do with the sun)-a star of its own and its light and warmth are necessary for life.

In the fourth and fifth lines he says that her stardust "has created a "celestial reaction" which has "captured" [his] "form"-he is hers. In the last four lines he says-"and vast as it may be [the universe]-the remaining nebulae (#45, 1. any of several light, misty, cloudlike,

61

patches seen in the night sky, consisting of groups of stars too far away to be seen singly, or of masses of gaseous matter)-not her special nebulae-"mean much less to [me]." Wow"!

Intangable [Intangible] Love [1973]
Intangable [Intangible] Love-not so
in afterglow [-] can leave
a melancholy soul [-]
Mellowed thing
Permcats a bring [?]
Alone reflected in each
breath nurtured
by sight and touch of
mind
K-73

Love between them seems intangible-(#46, pg. 759, adj. 1. that cannot be touched; incorporeal; impalpable. 2. that cannot be easily defined, formulated or grasped; vague). However, this is not so in the afterglow [of sexual union]-it is tangible but also "can leave/A melancholy soul"- Does he have that let down and feeling of separation afterwards that sometimes occurs? But at least this feeling is tangible. Next he pens "Mellowed thing"-Mellow is (#47, pg. 917, 2. full-flavored; matured; 3. full, rich, soft, and pure; not harsh…; 5. softened, and made gentle, understanding, and sympathetic by age and experience). This could be how he perceives her, how he perceives the sexual union, his own experience of the act, or any and all of these possibilities.

The fifth line of this poem-"Permcats a bring" [?] is unintelligible to me and the rest of the poem seems vague and disjointed too. The last four lines-"Alone reflected in each/ breath nurtured/ by sight and touch of mind"-Is his feeling of being alone enhanced by the awareness of each breath he takes? Is he nurtured by the memory of "sight and touch"-a product of his mind-the afterglow brought back to life again-temporarily refuting his alone-ness? This poem is a reminder of the few times it seemed Dad's brain had gone slightly off the rails. Maybe the title could have been-Intangible Poem.

It ['] s Grown to Be [no date]
It ['] s grown to be that the only
important things happen occasionally
Don't know what I ['] ve done for
you but I know what you have
done for me and [just] as
Brandy flowers good wine an[d] you
all belong on the same line.
No matter where I go they are
synonamous [synonymous] with a good life flow.

"It's grown" seems, to me, to be referring to an idea of Dad's that has blossomed, matured. This idea is that important things [events] only happen occasionally as compared to mundane things which happen frequently. Maybe as one ages, this becomes more the norm, in his view-as he has said "It's grown to be"-he grows into this reality or maybe he just becomes more aware. The rest of this sentence is-"that the only/important things happen occasionally" includes the word "only"-(#48, pg. 1025, adj. 1. alone of its or their kind; by itself or by themselves; sole)- the word "only" excludes all else. I think when he uses the phrase "the only important things…"

he implies, with this phrase, that occasional special times define their relationship [or not] and that the unimportant things that happen all the time don't matter so much.

This idea seems to stand on its own, for the next thing he comments on is about not knowing what he's done for her-because she doesn't tell him these kinds of things-but he proceeds to tell her what she's done for him. He then likens her to "brandy flowers good wine" and explains that she belongs on "the same line" with all these things-and they all are literally on the poem's same line- "Brandy flowers good wine an[d] you"

In the following last two lines he writes that he can be anywhere and conjure up these good things he mentions. They are, he proclaims, all "synonamous [synonymous] with a good life flow." So she, and these other important things he mentions-"brandy flowers good wine"- all meld together and create the epitome of the positive aspects of his life and he can go to them in his mind as he chooses, creating a "good life flow".

On Loving [no date]
A little at a time you
have come to dominate my
heart and mind.
Your constant sight has been the seed.
Consumated [Consummated] thing don't
understand your power
Your haunting refraine [refrain]
insane.

Dad writes in the first three lines that "A little at a time you/have come to dominate my/heart and mind". The next two tell that her

"...constant sight"-meaning, I think, that she is always available for him to gaze upon or possibly, he speaks of her uncanny insight. And so, either way, she is mesmerizing to him-the seed of his devotion. In the sixth line he calls her "consummated thing". The definition of consummated is "to bring to completion or fulfillment" (#49, pg. 317). The definition of thing (#50, pg. 1515) is 4. "that which is conceived, spoken of, or referred to as existing as an individual, distinguishable entity a) distinguished from all others". Next, he describes her influence over him-"...[I] don't/understand your power/Your haunting refrain". Haunting is "recurring in the mind; not easily forgotten (#51, pg. 664). This is the effect she has on him. He can't get her out of his mind. The word "haunting" is paired with the word "refrain". Refrain is (#52, pg. 1222) to hold back, curb an impulse-especially when provoked. Here he is describing Mom's quiet, though not always tolerant, nature. He is quite the opposite, so I suspect this nature of hers is perplexing to him and might be "haunting" because it is so foreign to him. However, as he couples the two words, her refrain is also her power over him. She keeps things to herself- secret. This makes her dangerous for him because he is haunted (obsessed with her) and wants to understand her but never really able to. He ends with the one word-"insane" in this final one word line-insane that she is this paradoxical way and/or insane because that's what he feels himself to be in her presence.

What Shall I Say [K-73]
What shall I say or show that
I care to expose heart and mind [']s
affairs.
Words [,] a light touch-

perhaps best that
eye [-] shine telegraphs the
message from my mind.
May I possibly than [then] choose
all three as a gift from me
If by a quirk of fate am
not alone when touched so
Tenderly by fate.
K-73

In this poem Dad starts out with an attempt to express to her his feelings for her and to ask the question-"What shall I say [to you] or [how shall I] show [you] that/I care [and want] to expose [my] heart and mind's/affairs." He presents two avenues he can use to communicate-saying or showing that his goal is to "expose [both] his heart [feelings] and "his mind's affairs." One definition of affair is (#53, pg. 24, 3. any matter, occurrence or thing). It is all these things that occupy his thoughts along with his feelings that he hopes to disclose to his beloved-both what's in his heart and mind.

Next, he explores other considerations and options. What will he say to her? How will he speak his mind? In what ways will he use all his resources? There are "words [and with them] a light touch-/ perhaps best that/eye shine telegraphs the/message from my [his] mind." His touch might communicate his affection. Better yet, is that "eye shine"-that special look in one's eyes that "telegraphs" adoration and ardor. I think here he uses the word "telegraphs" to emphasize this non-verbal communication just as a telegraph does. His eyes "speak" to her in that unspoken language, a mental telepathy. This touch and eye shine also suggest his interest in an intimate sexual union. Next he asks himself, in fact, wants to give himself permission to choose all three of these ways to communicate to her-words, actions, and "eye shine"-"as a gift."

In the last three sentences he questions how all this might come about. It will take "a quirk of fate"-If destiny-what is outside of his own volition-cooperates. In fact, if this quirky twist of fate occurs-if he is "touched so tenderly by fate" then all three aspects of his communication will "expose [his] heart and mind's affairs" with words, a touch, and eye shine. All three will accomplish his aim to establish a mutual relationship with her. In his dream she will return the favor and reveal herself to him and also desire a sexual union.

Here again, in this poem, he describes a power outside himself that he is beholden to-fate. There is also his trepidation about how she might really receive him, not just in his fantasy. And then there is his ongoing dread that his loving gestures will be met with less than he was hoping for.

Fantastectasy [K-73]
Watch T-V's idealistic caress [,]
[a] Gentle kiss [and] eyes [that] burn with [a lover's] idolatry.
Suddenly your motions [,] like a
symphony [,] rush to my memory.
Followed by a wish-a single
light kiss to transfer imagry [imagery][into]
Tender reality.
Then a slow light brush of
your cheek or mouth emoting
effectively [.]
A nod hand squeeze part and

emerge to fantastectasy.

K-73

In this poem Dad's title is "Fantastectasy." He combines the two words-fantastic and ecstasy- by leaving out the first "s" in the word ecstasy and the "ic" in fantastic to create his title. The definition of fantasy is (#54, pg. 526, adj., 1. existing in the imagination; imaginary; unreal. 3. thought of by unrestrained fancy; extravagant; capricious; eccentric; a lack of restraint in the imagination) These characteristics all seem to reflect Dad's flights of fancy. The definition of ecstasy is (#55, pg. 459, 1. a state of being overpowered with emotion, especially joy; being beside oneself with feelings. 2. a feeling of overpowering joy; great delight; rapture. 3. a trance). Thus, his ecstasy originates from his fantastic musings and this creates his fantastectasy-fantasy that is also ecstasy.

He starts out in the development of this state of mind watching the television with its "idealistic caress". Idealism is (#56, pg. 720, 1. behavior or thought based on a conception of things as they should be or as one would wish them to be; idealization). He finds this in the television's portrayal of reality in an idealistic lens. It is described in the poem as an "idealistic caress" because its portrayal is seductive and likely to have one formulate an unrealistic slant on life. His mind's eye sees a "gentle kiss", "eyes [that] burn with idolitry [idolatry]. Idolatry is (#57, pg. 722, 2. excessive devotion to or reverence for some person or thing).

The television show leads to musings and daydreams. He sees the TV's "idealistic caress/Gentle kiss eyes burn with idolitry [idolatry]. He imagines that this scenario could happen for him and leads to his own daydreams of his beloved. His mind's eye "Suddenly sees

[her] motions like a symphony [that] rush to [his] memory", her gentle kisses and her burning love-eyes. The two images meld-the television show and his musings about her.

In the sixth through ninth line he tells the reader that his musings are "Followed by a wish-a single/light kiss to transfer imagery to/ Tender reality"-he hopes this fantasy will become reality. He goes on with his daydream-"Then a slow light brush of/your cheek or mouth emoting/effectively"-he imagines all these gestures of her affection that become real in his mind, then "part" which returns his yearnings again to "fantastectasy"-a supreme pleasure all of the mind's making. Emoting is (#58, pg. 475, to conduct oneself in an emotional or theatrical manner). He hopes she will, at some point, in reality, be ardent.

Was Dad alone in some hotel room during one of his medical trainings, watching some romance on television, when he wrote this poem? Or was he in front of the T.V. in our family room in his red leather chair, next to Mom in hers-he, with his secret fantastectasy going on inside his head, and she, oblivious to it all? Or would his fantastectasy become his reality?

Just Because [3/18/74]
Just Because
You are part of me
Heart and soul of me
Absence felt
Immediately
Come back
resume your piece
of me.

This poem was written on what looks like a card that often accompanies a gift of flowers. In this case, it seems, the flowers were sent to Mom while she was away and he was at home. The sentiment expresses deep-felt love and adoration-"You are a part of me/Heart and soul of me" which makes his separation from her all the more difficult. Her "absence" [is] felt/immediately by him after her departure". He beckons her to return-"Come back"-for then she can "resume [her] piece of [him]." He wants her to claim him as her own. It seems that whenever they were apart it was difficult for both of them, but Dad was much more likely to be the one to be demonstrative about it.

Coast Collection-1. Grease/2. Gulls/3. Dust/4. Flaws [10-74]

Grease [1]

Grease is of little concern

Solidifies in any urn and

Scoops out great so why belly ache

Peace here is the deal of appeal

To nit [-] pick about grease is unreal

Was fun to pen this rebuttal

Because the view is the whole bubble

Each has a rainbow you know

In this poem Mom and Dad are at their beach place. In the first three lines he makes an entreaty for her not to spoil their time together with insignificant complaints-in this case, it seems, she is complaining about her difficulty in disposing of cooking grease. Dad starts out "Grease is of little concern/ [because it] solidifies in any urn." The reference to the urn may suggest one used for ashes of the dead-the grease is then laid to rest. Does this suggest that preoccupation with such trifle things is a form of being dead? He playfully adds that, after being placed in the urn, grease "solidifies" and thus "scoops out great so why belly ache." It becomes a non-issue, in his mind, because the grease is easy to manage.

In the fourth line there is a shift to what he thinks she is missing out on. "Peace here is the deal of appeal"-an appeal he makes for her to relax and enjoy their surroundings. Then he adds-"to nit-pick about grease is unreal"-hard for him to believe. Next, he tells her it was "fun to pen this rebuttal"-I wonder if she was amused. I doubt it.

The last two lines become more philosophical. What's really important here? Is it left over grease or "the view"-"the whole bubble"? I wonder if bubble is an allusion to all of nature-the world-round in shape and worthy of admiration and what is truly important. In fact, he states that "the view is the whole bubble"-it represents all of nature and the mystery beyond. He ends with his conviction that "each has a rainbow you know"-for a rainbow represents nature's beauty and mystery-maybe even "somewhere over the rainbow"-immortality. If one frets about insignificant things such as grease in this case, then instead of focus on the rainbow outside one's window, there is a form of a death all its own with this missed opportunity.

Gulls [2]
Gulls ever glide past
Constantly searching the sea
Serenity
Waves constantly rush ashore
Green white gray
possibly forevermore
Unique combination seen but once

by few purchased ashore
near Overlook view
joy ensue [s] [,] bursting to
Tranquility
fleeting seldom virtue
Found
here where its presence surrounds.

In this poem, as in many others, Dad's sensual awareness and joy in it is apparent. I think, in particular, he had an affinity for the sea, as do I. He speaks of the scene outside the picture window-"Gulls ever glide past/Constantly searching the sea/Serenity/[then] Waves constantly rush ashore/Green white gray/possibly forevermore"-first there is the calming hypnotic sight followed by turbulent beauty. This scene has him mesmerized by its seeming endlessness, maybe its everlasting constancy. There is a slight shift, then, in line seven, a counterpoint to the previous notion. All of what he witnesses-the gulls, the waves, are at that precise moment he witnessed them-a "unique combination seen but once"-will never again be just as they are now. He goes on to say that this unique view will be witnessed "by few purchased ashore/near overlook view." Purchased may mean what was paid to buy or rent a place for the privilege of having access to such a view, and this unique view only seen by a few within the vicinity of Dad and Mom's beach place. Further down the shoreline would produce another unique scene. Is this reminiscent of the different way people see things depending on their circumstances? I also wonder if the word "purchased" may also allude to the word perched. This would be in reference to the homes and rentals "perched" high up on the cliff as they are in this section of the coastline-"Unique combination seen but once/by [the] few [perched] ashore"? Dad often played with words this way.

"Joy ensue [s]" after witnessing this scene he describes, and then "bursting to/Tranquility"-the scene has led to "bursting", indicative of excitement, but then leads to "Tranquility" [that is fleeting] and the next two words that share line twelve with the word "fleeting" are "seldom" and "virtue" but I believe they also belong to the one word of the thirteenth line-"Found"-"Tranquility [is] fleeting" and virtue [is] "seldom/Found" It seems there are numerous possibilities in organizing the words related to capitalization, lower case, word order and meaning. The two words "Tranquility" and "Found", both capitalized, form the simple statement-"Tranquility [is] Found" (lines 11/13) or, as mentioned, one might say-"Tranquility [is] fleeting [and] virtue seldom /Found" and so tranquility is not necessarily virtuous (efficacious, syn.) It can't be trusted to last (lines 11/ 12/ 13 with transposing of the words virtue and seldom). Yet another option is "Tranquility/ [is] Found/here where its presence surrounds" (lines 11/13/14)-it can be as simple and in the moment as that. The separation of the words, with spaces between the three words in line 14, mimic the slow feeling of tranquility found where he is-in its presence [tranquility] that "surrounds" him.

Dust [3]

Dust [poem 2]

Stardust formed [,] cosmos born

Your special stellar dust

In celestial reaction has

Captured my form and vast

as they may be [,] the remaining

nebulae mean much less

to me

Dust ? [poem 1]

Stardust formed cosmos

born of your special

sellar dust.

In celestial reaction

has captured my form

and vast as it may be

The remaining nebulae

Mean much less

to me

When first I read this poem I thought to myself–"this really sounds familiar"–like something I'd read earlier on. So I looked back through the poems I'd already read and written about and, sure enough, there was the one titled "Dust?" several pages back. What surprised me was that when I read through "Dust" it sounded, almost word for word, like what I remembered from the first poem–and it almost was, but not quite. For one thing, Dad deleted the question mark in the title of this second poem and there were just a few other slight changes that could have been missed. Did he rewrite this poem unaware of the first? Did he remember it by heart and make deliberate changes? Or did he have the first right in front of him and then rewrote it? I'll never know. What I can do, though, is comment on the changes he did make. There was the question mark in the title that he eliminated, suggesting he is more firm in his conviction about this second poem's validity and its significance. Or was the first poem intended to be just a first draft, with his intention of going back to it and making improvements with a second version? Again, I'll never know. I include the first version after the second above for clarification in this discussion. Dad made changed in the line formation which, I feel, improved the second poem in some ways. There was also a change in the metaphysical content between the two.

In the earlier version [Dust?], Dad's first lines read–"Stardust formed cosmos/born of your special/sellar dust. I will repeat here, in part, what I wrote about this poem earlier on. Dad often speaks of universal concepts-romance, magic, the ethereal. His scientific schooling-mathematics, physics, chemistry, biology also influenced his belief system. This poem is full of cosmic words and phrases. Cosmos is the universe-considered to be an orderly and harmonious system-opposed to chaos-the disorder of formless matter and infinite space; supposed to have existed before the ordered universe. (See footnotes). The question mark in the title lends itself to the mysterious, the unknown, the elements of all. Also, in this poem, there is a period after the word "dust" which seems to connect the first three lines to one thought. However, the rest of the poem's lines also remain connected to the first three in thought, despite the period. The whole poem can be read as if it is one sentence. Stardust is the elemental building block of the cosmos and the second and third lines–"born of your special sellar dust" suggest that the cosmos was born (evolved) from his lover's "special sellar dust"-implying that she is the causal property of the universal-his universe. Also, the word sellar may be a combination of the words solar and stellar-both are similar; the first ascribes to our sun and its solar system, an essential to life on earth, and stellar alludes to all the stars in the universe. In the fourth and fifth lines he says that her stardust has created a "celestial reaction" which has "Captured" [his] "form"-he is hers. In the last four lines he says-"and vast as it [the universe] may be/The remaining nebulae [not hers]/Mean much less to me". For him, she is the only really important aspect of creation.

In contrast, the later poem's first line is "Stardust formed [and] cosmos [was] born"-here the stardust gave birth to the cosmos and this line stands alone even without a period at the end-the preamble. The rhyming element of the four words helps create this cohesion. The remaining six lines form one idea. The second line provides the subject matter-"Your special stellar dust", then moves to the adjective-"in celestial reaction ", then the verb-"has/captured" to the object-"my form" and finally to the result-"and vast /as they may be [,] the remaining/nebulae mean much less/to me". In this poem, the phrase reads "…vast/as they may be…", rather than "it may be" in poem 1. "They", here, refers to nebulae, but "it" in the first poem, refers to the universe. Here, after the subject line [2], subsequent lines connect the last word of the line with the first word of the next line. For example, line three ends with the word "has" and the first word in line four is "Captured", resulting in the melding of the two lines with the phrase- "has/Captured". Similarly, the end of line four ends "and vast" leads to "as they may be" at the beginning of line five. Then the end of line five-"the remaining" connects to the beginning of line six-"nebulae" The rest of line six-"means much less"-leads to line seven-"to me". I think this technique led to the poem's unified seeming message and creates a different type of cadence. If his second version of the poem had been written without the last word or thought in a line leading to the next, the modified version would read as follows:

[Stardust formed cosmos born]
Your special stellar dust
In celestial reaction
Has captured my form
And vast as they may be
The remaining nebulae
Mean much less to me.

As it stands, it seems easier to follow with this format, but maybe that isn't necessarily what he wanted to do.

Flaws [11-74] [4]
What is this lack in me
Will time let me see
Or shall I keep my blindness
to reality.
taking it to eternity [?]
Should I dessert [desert] my ways
allow insight
to rip away this blight [?]
Make amends
See the light
Doing what is generously right
Allowing all in love's sight
to live demand free
happily

In true equality
Will it ever truly be [?]
K 11-74

This poem is the fourth of the Coast Collection. At least, I think so. Dad added the date 11-74, so I wonder if this might have been near the end of this particular beach holiday or possibly after their return home. The previous three poems have only the date as K-74. However, all four poems appear to have been written on the same sort of notebook paper or stationary and to have been cut to accommodate each poem. They were written a few months after giving birth to my firstborn.

"Flaws" starts out with a self-deprecating evaluation. Dad asks himself questions that represent disappointment in himself-"What is lacking in me"/ [then] "will time let me see/or shall I keep my blindness/to reality"-even "taking it [his blindness] to eternity [?]"-he questions whether he will ever get it right in this lifetime of his and wonders if his blindness might even follow him beyond the grave. Although there is a period after the word "reality" in line four, the fifth seems to be a continuation of the question he asks himself-"…shall I keep my blindness/to reality/taking it to eternity [?]

In the sixth line there is a shift. He asks himself what, if anything, will change him for the better-"Should I dessert [desert] my ways/allow insight/to rip away this blight." The word blight (#59, pg. 156) is interesting to me. One definition of the word is- 4. "a person or thing that withers the hopes or ambitions of another person", another- 2. "to destroy" and a third- 3. "to disappoint or frustrate". Maybe all these definitions apply. Dad may have seen himself as the one who unintentionally harmed others with his ways, and thus, in the process, harmed himself. He, too, suffered. I know he was often quick to anger, criticism, and hubris. Maybe it was during this time in his life that he became more self-aware. But then, underneath it all, there was, from the beginning, and way down deep, his belief that he was no good. I believe it all had to do with his ethnicity and immigrant family, and trying to come to terms with fitting in.

But let's get back to the poem. He comes up with ideas to make a change-deserting his ways, "allow[ing] insight" (perhaps represented in this poem), and "… rip [ping] away this blight"-all are questions he asks himself. He goes on with ideas for change-"Make amends/See the light/Doing what is generously right/Allowing all in love's sight." He goes on-"to live demand free/happily/In true equality." I think he means that he might rid himself of feeling he has to prove himself as worthy and also accept others as they are. Instead he will live "happily/in true equality [with others]." The last line of the poem has him asking himself-"will it ever truly be [?]"-Will he be able to transform himself into this person he hopes to be? I was particularly taken with his choice of the "generously" in line 11. Definitions of generous (#60, pg. 603) are 2.noble-minded; gracious; not mean; magnanimous, 3.willing to give or share; unselfish; bountiful; liberal)-all lofty and admirable characteristics to aspire to.

I can't help but think that this poem relates, in part, to the first poem of the Coastal Collection-"Grease". Grease, if you remember, is about Dad's frustration with Mom's preoccupation with how to dispose of cooking grease. When I read this poem for the first time, I suspected that it didn't go over well with Mom. Mom and Dad were very different in many ways, but both had a propensity for fastidious obsessing. So Dad criticizing Mom's preoccupation, in my estimation, was rather hypocritical. What I suspect he came to at the end of this coastal holiday, is that it wasn't necessary to write such a poem as Grease-that it represented some of what he describes in "Flaws"-his flaws that get him into trouble. And in this poem he yearns to have insight about his foibles, make amends, and learn to make transformative changes to his personality which will benefit himself and his loved ones. The question is-in his last line-Will it ever truly be [?]

The next two poems-"In Spring" and "28/3-29-75/30/And More" almost seem to belong with the Coastal Collection. The first-"In Spring"-(written sometime in 1974- presumably after their stay described in the previous poems) doesn't take place at the coast but the stationary seems to be the same as that of the four Coastal poems). Dad writes of his nostalgia about their beach vacations at their special place and wonders when they will return and how long this will all last. In "28/3-29-75/30/And More" the two have returned in March of 1975, a few months after their last stay in November of 1974.

In Spring K-74
Will we be there again
That high place.
Sun and view [,] bottles of wine
we two – dream and joyfully
chatter of winter gone
summer yet to be.

How long will fortune stay [?]
repeat - repeat again – again
and still once more.
Then possibly above at timeless
equal intervals knowing no more
joy than we share now when
our eyes meet in some
selected retreat
to share at once an entire
entwined past.
No other way exists more
perfectly for two.
K-74

As mentioned above, in this poem Dad writes about their special beach place-Just the two of them there together again. Spring-time may be approaching, so he begins to reminisce about past pleasant visits there. He asks himself-"Will we be there again/That high place [on the cliff]." The title "In Spring"-does it represent new life and new beginnings? Dad pens fond memories-"Sun and view [,] bottles of wine/we two - dream and joyfully/chatter of winter gone/summer yet to be"-here, he describes an interlude between the seasons of winter and summer-spring. There is question about this "dream". For now it seems it will go on forever but he asks-"How long will fortune stay/repeat-repeat again-again/and still once more." The word formation of these repetitive lines mimics time's elusive nature. There seems a sense of mortality, and sadness with the thought that all these getaways will, at some point, end for them, and at the very least, never be quite the same again.

What will have become of the sun, view, bottles of wine, dreams, and joyful chatter?

In line 10, focus of the poem changes-"then possibly above at timeless/equal intervals…" I think "above at timeless equal intervals" and in "that high place" [perched high up on the cliff] both allude to the heavenly everlasting and the similarly eternal mark these getaways represent for them as a couple and that weave into the eternal fabric of All. Their holidays offer serenity, beauty, intimacy, and a glimpse of eternity. "Timeless equal intervals" it seems, suggests a difference from temporal time-there are no lapses or distinctions in a timeless realm. Similarly, they will "…share at once an entire/entwined past". This theme reoccurs in other of Dad's poems, in particular, his beach poems.

He goes on-even eternity will provide "…no more/joy than we share now [on earth]." This eternal state of theirs is described- "when/our eyes meet in some/selected retreat [a future getaway or in the afterlife]/to share at once an entire/entwined past"-all will meld together, and "no other way exists more/perfectly for two."

Some portions of "In Spring" are similar to the pattern seen in "Dust"-the last part of one line leads to the beginning of the next in part of each poem. "In Spring", lines 3 through 7 and 11 through 20, connect the last part of a line with the beginning of the next. These two sections would read as follows if written in a more conventional manner:

[Will we be there again]
[That high place]
Sun and view
Bottles of wine we two

Dream and joyfully chatter
of winter gone
summer yet to be.
[How long will fortune stay]
[repeat - repeat again – again]
[and still once more]
Then possibly above
at timeless equal intervals
knowing no more joy
than we share now
when our eyes meet
in some selected retreat
to share at once
an entire entwined past
No other way exists
more perfectly for two.

Again, I think the poem is easier to follow in this format.
28 3 -29 -75 30
And More
Eat drink read the news
View the ocean chase the blues
Sip more beer records soar
above the ocean [']s incessant roar
Sun and run for exercise
Floated beautiful Kites in
azure skies
Departed and started to reminess [reminisce]
About a return to all this

This poem has the dates of the holiday in a cross-shaped "t" as part of the title. The exact dates are March 28th, 29th, and 30th of 1975. The rest of the title is "And More"-additional days spent. In the last poem-"In Spring"-Dad is wondering if he and Mom will ever return to their beach spot. And guess what? They did. The stay, consisting of the three days plus mentioned in the title, seems to have been a success. He pens about their typical beach activities-"Eat drink read the news/view the ocean chase the blues/sip more beer records soar" and all this takes place "above the ocean [']s incessant roar" Next he tells of more fun-"Sun and run for exercise/Floated beautiful Kites in/azure skies" But finally, there is another departure with its melancholy, which leads to Dad's predictable reminiscing about this getaway and others that he hopes will follow. And they return-time and time again-but then finally it ends for them-old age sets in, and then death.

There's a record player, the old fashioned type, in most of the units at this beach place, with old albums often from Mom and Dad's era. And even though the ocean's roar is never ceasing, the music from the records "soar". It seems this suggests that their private life is significant in spite of the enormous influence of nature, in this case-the oceans "incessant roar." In the end, when the place is no longer inhabited by its occupants, the music from the records will cease. But for now, while they occupy this space with their human presence, that, like the ocean's roar, may leave its eternal mark. And I am always, when in this special place, in touch with the magic and mystical spirit of the place. Ghosts remain in these confines, or at least they visit, and I feel my parents' presence every time. They aren't the only visitors though. Each unit has journals for visitors to pen an entry. Many voice their conviction that it is a spiritual place. Some pour their hearts out in these pages. I have come to know them through their writing, and sense all these visitors' presence, along with my own family's presence.

Review [K-75]

Twenty five years spent by two

Now in melancholy review

Spin planet on time

I remain sublime of mind

Content in the past

Knowing the future can't promise

or possibly hold the

pleasures the past has allowed to unfold

Where will the next twenty five lead

Don't really care

Have had my share

But

there may still be

further revealing of minds

Wine-picnics-dinners with you

Christmas, Easters and [Catholic] masses for two

A toast

Oh - future allow

the children to see

the fate time held for me

K-75

This poem was written about the time of my parent's twenty-fifth wedding anniversary. Dad starts out describing what will be reviewed in his mind-"Twenty five years spent by two"-and, in the second line, reveals it is a "melancholy review". In line three he sees time as a "spin [spinning] planet on time"-the spinning creates the illusion of time with daylight, darkness and such. Next, in lines four and five, he describes being sublime (# 61, pg. 1452, 3.elated; joyful) of mind/Content in the past"-then turns his thoughts to the future-"Knowing the future can't promise/or possibly hold the/pleasures the past has allowed to unfold" The word "allowed" seems to allude to the concept of fate. Indeed, in the next line, he asks where the next twenty-five [years] will lead. Does he have any influence over the outcome or not? Then, in lines ten and eleven, he states-"Don't really care/have had my share" [of good times]. He doesn't want to be greedy even if much of the good in his life remains in the past.

The next one word line-"But" shifts the focus of this poem and offers a bit of hope for the future. The next six lines that follow speak to the possibilities-"There still may be/further revealing of minds/Wine-picnics-dinners with you/Christmas, Easter, and [Catholic] masses for two"-I note, especially, the line "further revealing of the minds" for he always wanted to be understood by Mom and to understand her. This involved lengthy conversations, the most private, intimate, personal thoughts and feelings shared-at least that was his hope. He makes "A toast" to all this in the next line and adds "Oh- future allow/ the children to see/The fate time held for me" Here, again, fate is mentioned, but instead of what fate holds in line seven, here, he writes "the fate time held"-the past tense. He pleads with the future to allow his children to see the fate the future held-for the word "held" implies a fatalistic view and his assurance that he will not be one to know this for himself.

If his children survive him, they will be the ones who know how the future dealt with him.

I find it interesting that he expressed this desire for his children to witness his days to his end on earth. We all did, and it wasn't easy. Maybe he had a premonition long before his earthly demise. Why was it so important for us to see it through? Did he see ahead that he might lose insight but that we would retain ours? Did he hope we would be there for him, if necessary? Or did he just want to make some sort of example of himself-good or bad? Did he wish for us to live out our own lives to a ripe old age?-like a superb bottle of wine that only gets better, a superb bottle of wine is what he always cherished for a good part of his life, but not able to enjoy in the end.

Modern Flight [K-6-75]
Hey awake at night
with ever [-] slight uptight
While dual fancies bite
then build a bridge
with either
hand to the right
Closeness-
Go blight
Caresses make it bright
Wishes
Fulfilled tonight
K-6-75

Dad is in a plane at night. I'm unsure why he called the flight "Modern". Is it because flights he took during this time in his life had evolved into pleasant, high-tech experiences with great service? It did used to be that way. "Hey" is his first word in the first sentence of this poem. It lends itself an impression of his sudden awareness of coming out of a deep sleep, the next words-"awake at night." The first word of the second line- "with"-connects the second line with the first, for he is awake "with ever [-] slight uptight." The combination of "with" and "uptight" then becomes a rather unusual pairing, as one would usually say "I am uptight." But he is awake with "uptight"-a noun in this case rather than the usual use of the word as an adjective. Then the word has become his companion. As in lines 1 and 2, the second and third lines are connected by the first word in the second of the two lines-"with ever [-] slight uptight/ [All the] While dual fancies bite."

He has two notions or "fancies" that may be dueling in his mind. He often seems to use a word, such as "dual", that sounds like another-"duel" to extend the possibilities of meaning. In this case, he has two different (dual) "fancies" going on at the same time in his mind. So both words-dual and duel-can be meaningful in this context. These two "fancies" could have a "bite" because they are opposing each other. Another definition of biting (#62, pg. 26, ACT Thesaurus) is penetrating; keen, sharp) and the definition of keen (#63, pg. 311, ACT Dictionary) is intensity, acute sharp senses) so the "dual fancies" could also just be complimentary intense imaginings. Also, the word "bite" might refer to both imaginings (fancies) having a biting quality on him-how his conflicting imaginings affect him. Or "dual fancies" could be complimentary-two that work together to motivate him to action, for eventually, they "then build a bridge" (line 4).

We can only guess what the "dual" (or dueling) fancies are-fantasizing about romance? Is it about insecurity? Hope for intimacy? Fear of rebuttal? But then, in the fourth line of the poem a bridge is built-"then build a bridge"-the result of forces mentioned in the previous three lines. The result is action. Does one of his hands reach out to hers?-"with either/hand to the right [of him]/Closeness-/Go blight"-he extends a hand to hers and this results in "closeness" and the end of "blight".

Does he only imagine her there? One way or the other, there is, for him, the feeling of "Closeness" (line 7)-either real or imagined. Then in line 8-"Go blight"-his withering state is gone. It is replaced with real or imagined "caresses" (that) make (his mind) "bright" There is happiness for "wishes/ [are] "fulfilled tonight". It seems to me that she was actually next to him on the plane, but then, his fantasy often led him to the illusion of reality. This is one of many poems that pertain to his need for closeness and affection from his one true love, and on this particular night, his wish may have been granted.

To You [K-6-75]
Love
to [too] long
to [too] little
Said
to [too] late
of that which
dealt us kind fate
I
thank

you now
for [being] the ultra-
mate.
K-6-75

This seems to me a poem of regret and then redemption. Dad starts out with the one word line "Love"- the topic of this poem. Then he uses the word "to" [too] to begin the second, third and fifth lines, but spelled the word as "to" rather than the correct "too"-"too long/too little/said/too late" I believe he meant that he waited too long, said too little, and said things too late "of that which/dealt us [them] kind fate". Here he speaks of gratitude to the fates for all the splendid events and feelings of their bond. So because of his neglect in uttering his appreciation for their good fortune, now he will. He ends this poem with-"I/thank/you now/for [being] the ultra-/mate".

Flower [K 75]
Youthful bloom
offered accepted
Integrated over
the years
tender flower
Petals taken
softly
in hand.
then heart
carried
with
Tender intent
Intact

held close

one score

near ten

more

K 75

The flower in this poem is his wife. I suspect he was thinking of the rose, for it was his and her favorite flower. Dad reminisces about the "youthful bloom" [that was] offered [by her] [and] accepted [by him]". I suspect his reference to the flower is a symbol of the female sexual organ and the "youthful bloom" that was part of their first sexual union. It was offered to him and he accepted. The second and third lines-"Integrated over/ the years" speaks to their first sexual union melding with all the others to this point in their lives-creating a unified intimate reality. Then, starting in the fifth line, he goes on to liken his wife to a "tender flower"-maybe a matured version of the "youthful bloom" of earlier on. Next, he speaks of "Petals taken/ softly in hand"-gentle sexual caresses of his hand."

In line nine, he introduces the emotional aspect of their recent encounter-"then heart/carried/ with/Tender intent"-his heart [emotions] and "tender intent" mimic his caresses, for then he describes having such feelings for her as "intact (#64, pg. 759, uninjured; kept or left whole; sound; unimpaired)/ [and] held close" in lines 13 and 14. He is confident in their mutual devotion. In the last three lines, "one score/near ten/more", Dad speaks of the length of their commitment. "One score" is twenty years and "near ten more" will make close to thirty. When this poem was written, their relationship had been nearly that long. Their courtship began in

Love Poems and Obsession

1946, right after Dad got back from the South Pacific after WWII, and they were married September 3rd of 1949.

Come Alive [K-75]
Six thirty five – Come alive
Breakfast for four [,] later more
Add dishes to those behind the door
Hustle out water and run
The fridge is empty [,] no fun
Lug fruit, vegetables meat and more
Clean [them] all – clean [them] all
It ['] s later – lunch for the bunch
and an extra few – Out again
Bills, prancing, gymnastics too
Run around Run around it ['] s almost two
Hustle – Hustle – water and dinner anew
Out and in – in and out
Phone – Phone answer it please
Will there be [cocktails] for duo [?]
Quiet – Peace – maybe a moment
Dinner – Dishes – Garbage and more
Bath – Noise – Slam – Bark and Clang
In an [and] out – out an [and] in.
Workers come – Workers go
Can't sleep – Weary dreary
toss muscles ache
Six thirty five – Come alive.
K-75

1975 seems to have been a prolific time for Dad's poetry writing. My brother Doug was still in high school and my sister Nora was about eight years of age. I was married with a toddler and my sister Sandy was in college and then off to Europe. The gist of this poem was the hubbub, toil and trouble in the household that interfered with Mom and Dad's peace and alone time together. Dad was still working and the kids had to get to school so six thirty five was when the day began. The timbre of the poem sets the tone and mental imagery for the reader. There's also a humorous quality.

Before, when all three and then four of us kids- when Nora entered the scene in June of 1967- were still home, the disquiet was surely even greater, which sometimes led to angry outbursts from Dad. Anyway, I think the poem provides an accurate portrayal of our home life. We were all hearty eaters and rambunctious. In this poem there were four of us left at home-Dad, Mom, Doug and Nora. The day starts out with waking and breakfast-"Breakfast for four [and] later more [food preparation and meals]. Then-"Add dishes to those [hidden] behind the [dishwasher's] door."

The next line-"Hustle out water and run" is about getting up, watering the lawn-in those days hoses, watering cans and sprinklers were it-they had to be changed frequently-and then one was off and running to the next chore. The lines 5 through 9 return to the topic of food preparation-"The fridge is empty no fun/Lug fruit, vegetables meat and more/clean [them] all – clean them all"-all of this repetitive and often boring. This theme continues with the following-"It's later – lunch for bunch/and an extra few – Out again/Bills, prancing, gymnastics too"-the extra few were friends and drop-ins; then more demands-"Out again/

Bills, prancing [like dancing], gymnastics [that Nora participated in]." This poem continues in this vane to portray general chaos and noise in the household and finally Dad wonders-"will there be coctails [cocktails] for duo." He hopes for "Quiet-Peace-Maybe a moment" but then it all starts anew and finally it is the end of the day and he "Can't sleep – [is] Weary dreary/ [tosses] muscles ache" and then it starts all over again-Six thirty five - Come alive."

A note: I think the word "bark" in line 18 refers to someone griping, for they didn't have a dog at that time. Also workers coming and going in line 20 are maintenance guys Dad would hire from time to time. In general, this poem is about domestic mayhem and on this particular day, at least, there was no down time for the two.

Friendly Skies [K-5-75]
Many times
These skies were
coursed in unity
Was burgundy with company
Today in solitarity
It
Passed in routine pleasantry
none of
The usual revelry
No cementing verbal ties
nudge or caress
only drawing round each eye
as
thoughts trace old ties of

cruises through azure skies
so cheers
May our next trips be
Anyone you take with me.

K-5-75

This poem is reminiscent of "Modern Flight", but this time, for sure, he is flying solo. When he speaks of having "coursed in unity", does the flight portrayed in the earlier poem-when she may have been present-come to his mind in this poem? I do know that his time spent alone away from her is a recurrent theme of his. In this one, his thoughts turn to "burgundy with company." While "Today [he flies] in solitarity" which "passed in routine pleasantry." I believe that in his use of "solitarity" he is combining two different words as he has done before. They are solitary (changed to solitarity) and solidarity. Both words are relevant to his message, and solitarity (coined) is not technically a legitimate word. Both words fit his context though. Solitary is (#65, pg. 1388, 3. characterized by loneliness or lack of companions) and solidarity is (#66, pg. 1388, complete unity, as of opinion, purpose, interest, feeling, etc.), which speaks to his belief that he shares all this with her. There is "none of the usual revelry" on this flight-only pleasantry-a light sort of banter with others he occupies himself with. Nor are there the "cementing verbal ties"- reminiscing, engaging in inside jokes, shared confidences, and intimate verbal foreplay.

Neither will there be (on this flight) a "nudge or caress"- instead "only drawing round each eye." I suspect here he is admitting to drawing circles around the eyes of people or animals in the magazines available to him in his seat, in order to pass the time and amuse himself. He always was quick to put his pen to use-writing, drawing, doodling. And while he does all this, his thoughts "trace old ties [as his pen draws circles around eyes] of [past] cruises through azure skies [with her at his side]." Next, he makes a cheer to her (likely with a glass, in hand, raised)-"may our next trips be/any one you take with me."

The title "Friendly Skies" gives credence to the significance of his air travel with his favorite companion, and even in his solo flights; for then he has the time to reminisce about flights they took in tandem, and has the opportunity to conjure up day or night dreams about future flights they will take together. Even when she isn't with him, he still has the opportunity to share pleasantries and jocularity with other passengers, doodle in the magazines available to him, look out the window at the scenery, enjoy a drink and have a meal. It's all good.

If Not with You [K-76]
If not with you I
order
martini twist & olive
too.
What would you
Do. [?]
K-76

The previous poem was penned in May of 1975. Beneath it, in the poetry album, there is what appears to be a brief ditty on a small square scrap of paper. It looks as though it was cut in the desired shape to hold a little poem, such as this one. It is dated

[19]76 so could have been written between about seven months to a year and seven months after "Friendly Skies." Was it a sort of postscript of the preceding poem?–"If not with you I /order/ martini twist olive/too./What would you/do [?] Again, here, he is flying solo and thinking about her as before and wonders if she was flying solo, would she indulge in the same way he does.

Figment [K-75]
Scheduled mini airliner mandatory early arrival
Quiet time
three hours four beers two papers later
the urinal was my grand theater
then the lobby till quarter of nine
Retreat to the restaurant–just in Time
Ideal corner booth for two
Prime
Prawns a tenth of wine
Reflected
that just passed
was easy to see
that
During that interval
None seemed to posess [possess]
Or act like we two
then I knew
the corner booth
really held two
me and
the figment of you

Ten

The airliner is due. K-75

In this poem Dad sits in an airport somewhere waiting for his flight. He has to be there early-"…mandatory early arrival" for a "scheduled mini airliner." Here he finds himself with time to kill. It's "Quiet time"-he passes the "three hours [with] four beers [and] two papers…" which results in the need for a urinal which he describes as "my grand theater"-the highlight of his solitary wait. Then he moves to "…the lobby 'till ['til] quarter of nine" (I think he originally wrote "to nine" and wrote over the "to" with "of"- I think it sounds better too) and "retreat [s] to the restaurant-just in Time" to secure an "ideal corner booth for two"-I believe the word "Time" is capitalized because of the significance of the concept of time in this poem that becomes more apparent.

The eighth line in this poem is only one word-"Prime"-indicating that it is the best spot in the place-especially for two. The next line tells of his order-that the prawns cost only a tenth of the cost of the wine. Dad always enjoyed good wine, especially when shared with Mom. It was frequently an important aspect of his amorous rendezvous with her too. So now he is in his corner booth all by himself with his prawns and wine. Then the tenth line-one word only again-"Reflected." He had all the time in the world to think in his solitude and what he reflected on was "that [which] just passed [by]/ [It] was easy to see"-(then yet another one word line)-"That"- (to introduce and emphasize what he saw)-"During that interval [in his booth]/none [of the others] seemed to posess [possess]/Or act like we two"-Dad always felt that no other couple could compare to them. Next, in line seventeen, there is a shift in his focus-his fantasy turns to reality-"then I knew/ the corner booth/really held two" The word "two"-an echo of the same word three lines up. Then he confirms that the two were-"me and/the figment of you"

In the next one word line again-"Ten" [o'clock]-the spell is broken. His awareness of temporal time returns, and he takes leave of his other reality. Temporal is (#67, pgs. 1500, 1501, 1. lasting only for a time; transitory; temporary; distinguished from eternal. 2. of this world; worldly; distinguished from spiritual). And now, his solitude also returns, but his true fantasy of her presence in the booth with him is but his true reality-an annihilation of time-that she is with him always, eternally, and I do believe she was and is.

Rings [K-2-76]
Watching movies solitare [solitaire]
Softly drifting rings
that break
Gracefully floating
fleeting forms
Silently
Drift more
Your countance [countenance]
saw it appear
Drifting memories
By
Beautiful things
Just
like Rings.
K-2-76

Dad is "watching movies solitare [solitaire]-again, he is alone. This poem is about his cigar habit, for one thing. I think he got more out of creating smoke rings and watching them dissipate, than anything else involved in his smoking them. He goes on to describe his observance of them—"Softly drifting rings/that break/graceful floating fleeting forms/silently/Drift more"

In the seventh line there is a shift from his focus on his wondrous rings to her "countance" [countenance]. It seems to me that, as he has done before, his coined word-"countance" is a combination of countenance and constancy. Constancy is (#68, pg. 314, the state or quality of being unchanging; being steady in affections or loyalties. Constant is 1. not changing). Countenance is (#69, pg. 336, the way one holds oneself, demeanor; 1. the expression of the face. 2. the face; facial features; visage). Her face appears in the rings-"Your [countenance]/saw it appear/"-as he observes the drifting rings of smoke. He also recalls and even sees "drifting memories/ [made] by/Beautiful things [that occurred]/and they are "just like the Rings"-floating, drifting, fleeting, silent-a magical, spiritual journey. I do believe Dad was so intrigued with smoke rings because he likened them to the ethereal (#70, pg. 499, 2. very light; airy; delicate; 3. heavenly, celestial, not earthly) quality of his senses, not earthly senses, but rather, celestial (#71, pg. 235, 2. of heaven; heavenly; divine) senses-and his celestial senses define his conviction that his deep devotion to his one true love will live on forever. This poem carries the same sort of message that is in the last-"Figment"-this distinction between stark temporal reality and his own experience that he likens to the divine.

Life [K 4-76]
Quiet reigns
Smoke rings emerge
Gradually enlarge
as they move
ever more slowly away
Perfect symetry [symmetry] slipping
Gently developing
more beauty and form
stratify then drift
to blend imperceptably [imperceptibly]
Each
In its unique way
Unseen currents direct
their fate
Silently
we are born
thanks.
K
4- 76

Here is another poem about smoke rings. This time Dad starts out with his two word line-"Quiet Reigns." "Quiet" is his friend and predominates in his life, for it allows for reflection. The second line begins a new direction in the poem-"Smoke rings emerge" and then he observes and describes them in sequence. They "gradually enlarge/as they move/ever more slowly away/ perfect symmetry slipping/Gently developing/more beauty and form/stratify then drift/to blend imperceptibly." I believe the poem, to this point, depicts universal movement. First, quiet reigns before creative movement and then movement emerges "gradually enlarge[s] [and] move[s] ever more slowly away"- (then) It expands from the core (The Big Bang?) in perfect symmetry (order) slipping (#72, pg. 1372, to go quietly or secretly by passing gradually into or out of some condition), then "gently developing/more beauty and form"-an allusion to ever increasing evolutionary complexity." Quiet refers to both his reflective state of mind and what leads to movement, both in creation and his own insight.

In the next line-"stratify then drift"-it seems this may be a reference to the earth's layers forming-"stratify" and then to the continental drift with the word-"drift" Next, there is the phrase-"to blend imperceptibly"-to mix, merge, and mingle for the desired result, that is, ongoing creation. He adds the lines-"Each/In its unique way" which, I believe, suggests differentiation and individuality. And how is this accomplished? There is a clue in the next phrase-"Unseen currents direct/ their fate/Silently/we are born." They are the cosmic force that remains mysterious. And just as the rings of smoke move about and morph into unique shapes and entities, so do humans and all of nature-the evolutionary process, and more intimately, one's fate; "Silently" because we are born without awareness, and our fate is unknown. However, in his case, fate led him to his lover, and so in this poem, he thanks the fates for all that this pairing has provided him.

On 4-13-76 [4-13-76]

what more

could I do to show my great respect

for you.
a
59 R.C.
but it
was saved
for your
delight
at your pref. [preferred] height.
K

Near the same time that the previous poem was written, Dad wrote a message to Mom on a cognac brandy bottle label. He asks her the question-"what more could I do to show my great respect/ for you. [?]" Then he answers his own question-"a [19]59 R.C. [Roth Child]/ but it/was saved/for your delight/at your pref. [preferred] height. He signs the cognac label 'K'. This note tells me that, in some past romantic event, the two had shared such a bottle and that Mom was impressed with this aged version [1959] of the Roth Child Cognac-Cordon Argent. I suspect this led Dad to set aside one of these bottles, in his wine cellar-in our add-on bathroom in their bedroom suite, for a special occasion. There was a hatch under a carpet that led to the wine which was kept cool underground. What made this gift so appealing was that this cognac was of her "preferred height"-aged to perfection and maturity. And now they will savor it together, in this special similarly matured stage of their lives, and in honor of his respect for his beloved. Dad often spoke of this particular cognac with great relish, so that all of us kids knew his opinion about it.

My Prayer For You [K-76]
Please

Let time pass
to
wipe all sadness from your eyes
Time
bless with peace
set her mind at ease
Rest contented
New mind with inner bliss
Time
Then Transfered [Transferred] to
Bodily serinity [serenity]
Lord so may it be.
K- 76

In this poem Dad addresses Mom's internal torment. It seems that as their years passed, he became more aware of her struggles, or maybe her torment just intensified. First, he says a prayer for her to "let time pass" and "wipe all sadness from your eyes." This wish or prayer seems to be an entreaty to her directly. The first mention of time, in line 2, is not capitalized. I wonder if this is because he speaks of temporal time-her personal experience with it and his hope for her gradual working through of the reasons for her torment. His hope is that the outcome will be renewed well-being for her. Next, in lines 5 through 9, he addresses Time [capitalized] itself-I believe a reference to Cosmic Time. He asks Time to bless her mind with "peace", "rest", and "inner bliss." His third mention of "Time" comes in line 10, and again, the word is capitalized in this one word line. Now, time isn't addressed directly. "Time" is now only a vessel for her change. It will allow all that he hopes for her.

It will not only allow her a serene mind, but will be "Transferred to/bodily serenity" and he ends with a plea in this prayer in the last line-"Lord so may it be.

Airport Stay [K-12-76]
See the couples at the port
Watch them - Silent [-] sit drink and stare- Now
a New-engrossed pair [-] window seat abreast
Oh Joy. - Wait.
His hair is gray [-] her skin is white and fair
No bands lie there [-] no lasting
bond
It ['] s born to be short and physical I fear.
Another couple of similar vein - Bearded beau
and clinging packsack girl converse abreast
against the wall
Alas band [-] less all his composure cool
Un [-] commitment here I fear
More stare [-] some young [,] some old filter
in and out - an endless stream.
unless 2 couples or more share the surrounding air
See little there. But always nothing
from those not against the wall
Were [Where] do we sit in the prominade [promenade?]
Against the wall-laughing close bands and all. K-12-76
P.I.A.

Here is another airport/airplane poem where Dad observes his surroundings-in particular, other people. In his first line-"see the couples at the [air] port", he takes it a step further in the second line. He watches one couple who is "silent sit drink and stare-"

(What would he think these days when everyone has a technical device in hand or in front of their eyes? Not much, I'll bet). Next, he spots "a New-engrossed pair window seat abreast"-sitting side-by-side in the terminal. He exclaims, silently to himself-"Oh. Joy. - Wait." These three words stand by themselves with the periods at the end of each word. "Oh." tells the reader that he sees something interesting and encouraging. "Joy" describes his delight that he may have spotted a couple worthy of admiration. And "Wait" tells the reader that he sees something that brings in doubt. Now, he notices the significant age difference between the two-"His hair is gray [,] her skin is white and fair"-the color of her skin suggests youth and inexperience. Next he notes that "No [wedding] bands lie there [on their fingers, so] no lasting bond [in their future]" -then he makes the assertion that "It ['] s born to be short and physical I fear", for this is a May-December coupling without true loyalty or devotion, in his estimation.

In the next three lines he spots yet "Another couple of similar vein - Bearded beau/and clinging back [-] sack girl converse abreast/against the wall"-the couple he observes stand "abreast against the wall" Does this stance suggest a lack of intimacy, eye contact? He adds that they are "Alas (his exclamation of sorrow or pity) band [-] less all his composure cool/un [-] commitment here" he fears. He deems this couple superficial too. Next, he makes another swift scan of the rest in the vicinity-"More starers [stare-ers]-some young [-] some old filter/in and out-an endless stream." His conjecture-they are all the same-staring ahead, without eye contact with others. They are lost in the crowd- the "endless stream." He continues to examine his surroundings and, again, makes observations that confirm his stance-"Unless 2 couples or more share the surrounding air/see little action there" They continue to all look the same to him. All these people share is the surrounding air [and he] see[s] little [action] there"-nothing of consequence, but at least they share something-air. He becomes even more convinced as he continues to peruse the area-"But always nothing/from those not against the wall." Dad makes some sort of distinction between people against the wall and those that aren't, but none of the couples he sees here seemed to have impressed him. I have puzzled over this distinction he makes and his final conclusion in this poem. But maybe if against the wall, as the second couple-"the bearded beau and pack-sack girl"- there may be some sort of courtship going on with the potential for a romance and a true commitment. Next he says-"But always nothing/ for those not against the wall"-why not? And he didn't seem all that enthused about this couple against the wall either. Finally, he asks the question-"Were [Where] do we sit in the promenade [?]" and he answers-"Against the wall-laughing close bands and all." They are against the wall (whatever that means) and they have what it takes, in his estimation. In addition, there is "laughing" between them-fun? delight? He is feeling confident, or even smug, about their relationship, and confident in their commitment to each other. Their wedding bands are a symbol of all that a marriage entails.

P.I.A. under the date at the bottom of the poem stands for Portland International Airport. This is the port that he, she or they usually flew out of to any number of destinations.

See [12-20-76]

Need me-

Spirit call me now

Out of that deep finanial [financial/fanatical/finical?]
Solitary ravine.
Where I have been.
Need me down in your hole
Could I be
Your magnetic pole-
the North-South all your soul
Need me alone-a day-two or three
My direction I pledge will be
magnetic true
Directly to you
K. 12-20-76

Dad starts this poem with a two word plea-"Need me"-the first line, followed by the second line-"Spirit call me now." The next four suggest that what he needs is to be rescued, maybe from himself. He may be calling upon a spirit to help him-his own or the spirit of another. He makes an entreaty to this spirit-"…call me now/out of that deep finanial [financial, finical, fanatical]/solitary ravine." I wonder about his use of "finanial". Could it be a combination of similar sounding words that all relate to the meaning in the poem? As mentioned, he often did this kind of thing in his poems. Dad often studied over his financial investments, the stock market, etc., in his easy chair in our family room. He describes his condition as a "solitary ravine" for one thing. Did he get too obsessed and bogged down in all of it? If so, all these similar words can apply. He could be describing himself as finical (#73, pg. 544, fussy; fastidious) or fanatical (#74, pg. 525, overly zealous) about his financial pursuits. Maybe he was also just in one of his darker moods that seemed

Cheryl Krkoč

to him like a "solitary ravine"-ravine (#75, pg. 1208, a long deep hollow in the earth's surface), and then asks himself-"Where have I been."

In the sixth line, there is a shift away from his self. He goes back, and repeats "Need me" and adds to it-"down in your hole" but this time he seems to be speaking to another-the one he is writing the poem for. Is the word "hole" reminiscent of the word "ravine"? It seems he pleads with the other to "need" him-his only escape from his solitary ravine. Instead, he will enter into hers. Next, he asks-"Could I be/Your magnetic pole-/the North-South all your soul" (I wonder if the words hole and pole have a sexual connotation?) Could he be everything to her-all of her soul? And would this eliminate his despair? For the third time he writes "Need me" (line ten) but adds the word alone-"Need me alone-a day-two or three." He wants her to need only him. Or is it that when he adds "a day-two or three" he means that he wants to be alone with and all things to her, even if for a limited time, and even that would suffice. If his wish comes true then his "…pledge will be/magnetic true"-the magnetic force field is his emotional, spiritual, sexual energy-all directed to her. In the last two lines he promises that if she takes him up on his offer "My direction (like a magnetic pole) "…will be/magnetic true/Directly to you." His focus, energy, and attention will be hers alone-a far cry from "…that deep solitary ravine he is lost in now.

Nearness [K-4-77]

Think and dream

of you

intermittantly [intermittently]

The whole day through
Did you know
the only amiss is
simple nearness
Close to you don't need
verbal exchanges
Silence and proximity
alone produce
sublimity
Thanks.
K-4-77

This title of this poem is the subject- "Nearness"-a short and sweet poem. The first four lines describe Dad's day dreams-"Think and dream /of you/intermittently/the whole day through" Then he asks her a silent written question that remains in his own mind-at least until she reads it-"Did you know/the only [thing] amiss is/ simple nearness-her physical absence during his daydreaming. Next, he goes on to explain himself further-"[when] close to you [I] don't need [any]/verbal exchanges [because]/Silence and proximity/alone produce/sublimity" In the last one word line- "Thanks [for just being there]"-her simple presence means that much. But she was such a quiet person. Did he ever yearn for more than that?

Should Tell You [K-77]
Should tell you daily
love you
Easy thing to do
But routinized

Cheryl Krkoč

Drift along unverbalized-
Tragedy
Sudden shift
to [too] late [,] so great
is death ['] rift.
K-77

In this poem Dad starts out with a declaration of regret.- "Should tell you daily/[that I] love you" in the first two lines. Then what follows-"Easy thing to do/but routinized [becomes routine]/Drift along un [-] verbalized-/Tragedy"

His daily routine interferes with following through with his intentions. The two rhyming words "routinized' and "un-verbalized" are linked in cause and effect. The result, in his mind, is "tragedy" The last three lines sum it up-"Sudden shift/too late, so great/is death's rift." Is the "Sudden shift" one in his lover's feelings for him? Is it her disinterest or disillusionment? He thinks it's "too late" to repair the damage done by his inattentiveness-"so great/is death's rift." Is he speaking of the death of her feelings for him, the rift (#76, pg. 1254, n. an opening caused by or as if by splitting; cleft; fissure; crack; [for base see rive]). Rive (#77, pg. 1258, 1. to tear apart; rend; 3. to break or dismay the heart, spirit, etc.).

I also note the three words in the poem that rhyme and have an "F" in them-"Drift", "shift" and "rift". Instead of penning his usual cursive "F", he draws a straight line instead. "Drift" points downward to "shift" and "shift" points downward to "rift". The three words signify what he perceives as the sequential undoing of her love for him-it's death. Or maybe he speaks of the possibility of actual death leaving a rift-a consideration that might prevent

Love Poems and Obsession

tragedy if rectified soon enough–if he changes his ways and pays her attention.

Lined up a Place [no date]
Lined up a place to eat
Boston Huff Schnell –Sounded neat.
But the dinner did me in/ [before]
I ordered my first round.
Retreat [to] Ambassador [Hotel]
as I walked by [,] [it] seemed neat.
Beer #1 Palm Room one
look around [,] nostalgia
abound–Was a place for us
a coctail [cocktail] or two–before
a dinner you see.
The view at 82 was of
palms inside and out
Blooming flowers abound
missed you not around.
So had a martini
with twist & olive too
took a look around [,] not a
couple like us around.
Ambassador Lautrec 7:30
Believe it or not [it was] empty
save for me and a screened
off private party.

This is another of Dad's poems in which the topic is loneliness. It seems he must have been on some business meeting in Boston.

He "lined up a place to eat"-Boston Huff Schnell. He adds that it "Sounded neat", but it seemed to have been a disappointment.-"The dinner did me in/before I [even] ordered my first round." From there he "retreat [s]"-withdraws to a safe, secluded or private place, the Ambassador Hotel, and adds that as he "walked by, it seemed neat."-but then so did the Boston Huff Schnell initially. Here, too, he is alone. He has something more to drink- "Beer #1 [in the] Palm Room", then looks around, and finds that "nostalgia/abound [s]-Was a place for us"- for maybe they had been there together before, or at least, he deems this place to be somewhere they would enjoy together. He dreams about what it would be like for them to have a rendezvous at the Palm Room together –" [we would have] a coctail [cocktail] or two-before/a dinner you see." Next, he writes of "The view at 82 was of/palms inside and out/Blooming flowers abound/[and he] missed [her] not around." Was he on the 82nd floor? Was he at table 82? Would they both enjoy the flowers he describes if they were together?

He remains lonely without her "so [he] had a martini/with twist & olive too." Then he takes "...a look around [but] not a/couple like us around." He compares other couples unfavorably with them as he has in earlier poems. Finally, he has a solitary supper at Ambassador Lautrec at 7:30 P.M. In the last three lines of this poem he emphasizes his solitary state there at his table, and tells her-"Believe it or not [it was] empty/save for me and a screened/ off private party." The place was not lively as he might have hoped, which might have mitigated his loneliness. Instead, there is a stark departure from his fantasy!

Tide Out [2-7-77-9:00 PM]
Alone then three descend
One hundred steps to
night [-] time quiet beach

Above two stars shine through
thin whips of
air suspended dew
Along [with this] are lights up on
the hills
Both filtered through
Trees and dew
50[degrees] no wind at all
Ocean ['] s white cresting waves
Move
Four-five at a time ever smaller
toward shore
while
up on the hill
Smoke columns move
straight up
Are they fingers of praise
to one above.
K 77

This is another of Dad's beach poems. The beach is deserted-"Alone"-"[but] then three descend" and the beach is no longer alone. The three are Dad, Mom and ten year old Nora. They "…descend the hundred steps" that take them to the "night-time quiet beach" below the cliff our beach spot sits upon. The remainder of the poem describes the sensual and emotional aspects of Dad's sojourn. He creates a beautiful kinesthetic rendering of the night's excursion. Next, he writes-"Above two stars shine through/thin whips of/air suspended dew." This first observation focuses on the sky. The stars shine through the whips of dew suspended in the air. His next observation attends to lights-"Along [with the stars and dew] are lights up on/ the hills" and both sources of light-the stars and the artificial street lights and the abodes on the cliff-"... filtered through/Trees and dew." The third focus is to the weather and waves on the beach. He describes them as such-"50 degrees no wind at all/Ocean's white cresting waves/Move/four-five at a time ever smaller/toward shore"-he seems mesmerized by the sight. Then he moves to the hills-"While up on the hill/smoke columns move/straight up"-I can just see, hear, feel, smell and touch it all. Finally, he asks himself the question-"Are they (the smoke columns) fingers of praise/ to one above. It is as if the scene itself, taking on a human quality, is praising creation and the creator of such immense, immeasurable, limitless and infinite beauty. In this poem, as in others, there is the touch of the mystical.

[Taking] Sides [K 8-77]

Refused

a partnership lawyer post meeting dinner invitation

Traveled-

home in tired hasty anticipation

Did

I-We misinterpert [misinterpret] the intonation of my

mate ['] s initial incantation.

To

reply with rapid irrational irritation

Bilaterally

destroying the expected exhilaration.

Hurt

Both toss attempting a restless sleep

Dawn are

There minute possibly asymetrical [asymmetrical] repairs

Drawing

On past strength is the rent progressivly [progressively] resolving

Never

to completely fill again oh. Tiny scar

Toast

Past happy times –future hold more of the primes K8-77

In this poem, Dad describes the near end of a business trip and is eager to get home to his wife. He even "refused/ a partnership lawyer post meeting dinner invitation" Each segment starts with a one [or two] word line that introduces and defines the following line or two. In the first, he "Refused" the meeting to get home sooner. Next, he "Traveled"/home in tired hasty anticipation" The next one word line is "Did" which will be the start of a question he asks himself, and maybe her too-"Did/I-We misinterpret the intonation of my/mate's initial incantation[?]" One meaning of intonation is (#78, pg. 636, the rise and fall of pitch). Incantation is (#79, pg. 735, chanting of magical words or those casting a spell; sorcery). So, he first anticipates a warm homecoming because of her seductive spell-binding manner and sing-song words. But he is sadly mistaken. Was her tone of voice truly magical and glad, or is he detecting irritation in her voice now? Has he unwittingly misinterpreted her mood? The next one word line is "To" which prefaces a swift change in mood-he or they reply or react "with rapid irrational irritation". He goes on in the same vein in the next one word line-"Bilaterally", for this irrational irritation seems to have been created and felt by both of them. The result is a "destroying [of his] expected exhilaration" at his return home. The result is revealed in the next one word line-"Hurt" that leads to a sleepless night for both="both [of us] toss attempting a restless sleep". There is no romance in store on this night.

Next comes the only two word transition or connecting line of the poem, "Dawn are"- the beginning of a question he asks himself-"…are/there minute possibly asymmetrical repairs" that the dawn will bring? He looks for signs of some sort of possibility for reconciliation, even though it may be "minute". If so, it will be "asymmetrical", I suspect, because he thinks he will bear the burden of "repairs" to the relationship. Just how he will accomplish this goal is introduced in the next line-"Drawing"/on past strength is [the way] the rent [will be] progressively resolving". The "rent" is (#80, pg. 1232, 1. a torn place in cloth; 2. a breach of relations, schism). He asks himself if the strength of their relationship will pull them through this rift, but then, the next one word line-"Never" takes on another consideration. The following line finishes the thought-"Never/to completely fill again oh. Tiny scar" The "oh" is the sad recognition of what can not be saved and mention of a "tiny scar" is the sign of the stain on their bond. Some of the hurt will remain, for him, at least, the allegorical "Tiny scar" that may fade, but never completely vanish. The final one word line-"Toast" changes the tone of the poem. Toasting was a frequent occurrence in our family from way back. In this case he toasts "[to] past happy times-[and that the] future [will] hold more of the primes [prime times]" This sentiment echoes the mention of "drawing/ on past strength" to mend the damage done in hopes that the "future [will] hold more of the [prime times]-the best in life.

Thank You [K-10-77]
Thank you for being there
Thank you for the way you care
Thank you for what we share
Like the weekends at the beach
Coffee wine and coctail [cocktail] time
Quiet talks about the kids
in those active luncheon pits
Thank you for being here sweet one
I hold so dear
Thank you.
K-10-77

This poem was placed in the album a few months after the last. There is quite a change in tone (or should I say atone?) from the previous "Sides". Is this a conciliatory attempt on Dad's part? He thanks his mate "for being there [for him]" for the way she cares for him, for what they share. He goes on in the next four lines to provide examples of what they share-"…the weekends at the beach/Coffee wine and cocktail time/Quiet talks about the kids/ in those active luncheon pits." The "luncheon pits" is in reference to the commotion in our kitchen with its bar and stools used for informal midday meals-a pit stop, so to speak. Finally, he thanks her for just "being there", adding the endearing expression-"sweet one" and adding to it-"I hold so dear". Then there is the last line-only "Thank you".

Why [K-5-78]
Partially watch the crap on T.V.
Light a Parta gas [Partagas] and meditate

Wonder did I help you down
Think as I scan a financial sheet
How can I help – What can I do
Change my fibre [fiber]. Reshape the past
Possibly the former
Certainly not the last
Past seamed [seemed] right to me
but
did it help trigger your insecurity
Now what will the future bring
the good or bad for three.
We see no pleasure unless you are free
So
Cast the devil out to sea and
resume your usual tranquillity [tranquility]
Because
We are still entwined Nora you and me
in
mutual dependency.
K-5-78

The title of this poem is a question and as the poem progresses more questions are asked, only a few really answered. He ponders the difficulty in the household-Now only he, she and Nora are left. He puzzles over all this while "Partially watch[ing] the crap on T.V. Next, he will "Light a Parta gas and meditate" The Parta gas [Partagas] is a fine handmade Cuban cigar that Dad loved to smoke and make smoke rings with in front of the fireplace. He always did love the experience of the warmth that emanated from the dancing flames, and his smoke rings-mesmerizing to him, and likely conducive to the meditation he writes about here.

The third line contains the first crucial question-"Wonder did I help you down" he thinks "as I scan a financial sheet". His family room lounge chair, in front of the fire and the television, is where he did most of his financial scheming. But now, he will formulate an hypothesis for his questions about his wife-"How can I help-What can I do/Change my fiber/Reshape the past". He answers these questions in the next two lines-"Possibly the former"-(changing his fiber), but "Certainly not the last"-reshaping the past, for that ship has sailed.

In the ninth line, he provides a tentative defense of how he has lived life so far-"Past seamed [seemed] right to me" It looks as though he pens "seamed" rather than "seemed". I wonder if this was intentional, creating two different meanings in one. The definition of seamed is (#81, pg. 1314, 2. any line formed by the joining together of separate pieces). Hence, they were compatible, almost one. However, if the word seamed is replaced by seemed, then the conventional meaning emerges-"Past seemed right…" Seem is (#82, pg. 1319, 1. to appear to be; give the impression of being), which is what it seemed to him at the time. In the next lines, though, he questions his assumption-"but/did it help trigger your insecurity" –the crux of the matter-did their lifestyle and his ways contribute to her current condition?

The rest of the poem has him pondering the present and the future. In line 12/13 he asks-"Now what will the future bring/the good or bad for three"-himself, his wife, and eleven year old Nora. His prediction and plea to her-"We see no pleasure unless you are free [of torment]" Line 14 is the one word "So" which leads to his provisional conclusion-what she needs to do to fix things-"Cast the devil out to sea and/resume your usual Tranquility". His next one word line "Because" leads to the next three, explaining the need for her to change-"We are still entwined Nora you and me/ in/mutual dependency." In this last section of the poem he implies that evil (the devil) has taken hold of her. He implores her to "cast the devil out to sea", the image of water being a purifying symbol, where the devil is likely to drown if cast out. Then she would be able to "Resume [her] usual Tranquility". These last four lines decry her state of mind and imply its bad influence over the household. Sadly, I don't know that any change ever occurred.

Dear Heart. [K-78-6-6]

Love you In my quiet way

When you [are] near it's the best

of my day

Even though I may not have

The sense to say

Daily I feel closer to you

in every way.

That ['] s why I become sad

of heart even when

others part.

Remain K-78-6-6

my dear heart.

This poem was written not long after the last. The tone is different, but still tentative. He starts out-"Love you in my quiet way/when you [are] near it ['s] the best/ of my day." Again, as in other of his poems, he will admonish himself for neglecting to verbalize how he feels about her-"Even though I may not have/ the sense to say/[that] daily I feel closer to you/in every way"-but he is able to pen his sentiments.

There is a shift in the eighth line. He admits to emotions he has for others besides her. He admits to this sentimental nature of his when it involves others, but this may essentially be due to his feelings for her. She is the reason he extends to others his sadness at their departures-because he feels "closer to her/in every way."That [is] why [he] become[s] sad/of heart even when/others part." He ends with the line-"Remain/my dear heart"-for without that, he wouldn't have much to offer anyone else.

When [9-78]
How about a holiday
for two
With walk-and talks
hopefully
in the sun
Some shopping for
nicknacks
Leisurely noon time snacks
Breakfast at pool or
Oceanside
Rent a cycle go for a ride
The tempo will be slow
Say the word
and we will go.
Love

Bob

9-78

The title of this poem is a question. "When" might this happen. He makes a suggestion in the first line–"How about a holiday/for [we] two/with walk-and talks…" He goes on to suggest what they might do. Finally, after his rendition of this perfect getaway, he implores her"'-Say the word/and we will go. He signs off with "Bob"-short for his middle name Roberto. I wonder whether or not his entreaty was successful, and if they did, in fact, get away together. The benefit may not have been long-lasting, or not brought about his intended result based on the following poem. I do know that at some point, Mom refused to go with him to the family beach spot any longer.

Love You [K-11-2-78 x10]
As you are tonight asleep
Tired and distraught
Reposed at needed rest
Before our usual daily Tests
Routine
Does one down
at illness pleasure or at sin
acts that really never meet
mostly ends incomplete
Goodness scores in heart we know
So hail our status quo-
Oh to prognistications [prognostications] to
the better
to

greater days
than those ago
a toast to pleasures
that
count our past delights
Oh arise
A fresh miracle at noon
reborn [,] new [,] complete
fresh two.
K-11-2-78x10

I'm calling the title of this poem "Love You". However, as in many, what I choose as a title is sometimes really only the first line of the poem, as in this one. Dad pens "Love you/as you are tonight asleep". It seems he is the one aware and adoring her as she sleeps beside him. He writes that she has been "Tired and distraught/ [but now] Reposed at needed rest". "Before [her sleep there were their] usual daily tests/Routine/does one down" or gets one down. I believe here again, he is commenting on the struggle she has (or possibly both of them have) with routine daily living. He elaborates- "at illness pleasure or at sin/acts that never really meet/ mostly ends incomplete." I'm not sure about the meaning of these three lines, but I'll give a guess. What "does one down"/can be "illness, [even too much] pleasure or at sin [some misdeed]" so that "acts never really/ meet/ mostly ends incomplete"-Is it that routine, including illness, even pleasure, and sin-don't have to be connected. They are random events or actions, implying that routine has no direction or purpose.

The rest of the poem takes on a new temperament. It starts out- "Goodness scores in heart we know/so hail our status quo-"I suspect here he refers to both of their admirable qualities (goodness) and to their long history of relationship success together (our status quo). This beam of hope leads to the next line-"Oh to prognostications to/the better/to/greater days/than those ago/"-he wants to be able to predict a brighter future "than those ago"-Ago is (#83, pg. 28, what has gone by). His enthusiasm mounts –"A toast to pleasures/ that/count our past delights/Oh arise/A fresh miracle at noon". One definition of noon is (#84, pg. 1000, 2. the highest point or culmination; time of greatest power, etc.: as in the noon of his life) so he asks for this 'fresh miracle" at the pinnacle of their lives. Now, he hopes, they will be "reborn new complete/fresh two"-a fresh start for these two. He signs off K-11-2-78x10. The "78x10"- this year they are in now will be multiplied by 10 for a long and fruitful future.

Up Again [Kerk-1-79]
Makes me sad to see you down
Lacking your usual smile when
I come around
Bottom aching
Appetite not up to par
Turning down our usual lunches
In bunches
Different we two as night and day
But not in pride I must say.
Oh see our partnership
Don't depreciate your game

You are full of the stuff
Ladies and queens are made of
So I toast you my love
Like the Chinese on the boats
the lines and cards today
Say
Better eighties are on the way
So soon in a southern clime
God willing
We will have a close wonderful time
It says so in
your palm line.
Kerk-1-79

This poem was written in the first month of the New Year. Is good luck in a new year hoped for? But it starts out on a sad note- "Makes me sad to see you down/Lacking your usual smile when I come around." He notices not only her low mood but also her unresponsiveness towards him. Then he focuses back to symptoms of her malaise-"Bottom aching (she had a chronic urinary tract condition-cystitis that she suffered with for years)/Appetite not up to par/Turning down our usual lunches/in bunches"

In line eight the focus shifts back to observations of their relationship-"Different we two as night and day/But not in pride I must say." I think here he begins his argument about how, although they are different, they are both prideful in their own way. Next, he seems to elaborate on her pride in a positive light. He asks her to take a look at their relationship-"Oh see our partnership"-that she has more power in it than she realizes-"You are a full of the stuff/Ladies and queens are made of/So I toast you my love". He tells her here that she is strong willed and majestic in spite of her seeming fragile demeanor. Then "Like the Chinese on the boats/the lines and cards today/Say/Better eighties are on the way" He likens her to brave ones who travel by boat, in treacherous conditions, to find a safer place. There is also an allusion here to Chinese New Year fortune cookies and newspaper headlines which predict good fortune in the new year-"The lines and cards today/Say/better eighties are on the way" This poem was written in January of 1979 with only a year before a whole new decade would emerge, but he anticipates a positive change even sooner in this new year-"So soon in a southern clime/God willing/We will have a close wonderful time/It says so in/your palm line." He is planning a trip "in a southern clime" to boost her mood. He practices, at least in his mind, palm reading that predicts his wishes to come to fruition, but it is her palm that tells the future, for he is only the one interpreting it. He is the one with hope. The reader knows not what she hopes for, if anything. But for him, it is that she will be "Up Again". He signs off "Kerk", one of his nicknames.

[1-27-81]

Was an interesting day because
I got to stay. at the hospital
for a prolonged delay.
It was only an inconvenience for me
Because all I had to do was stay.
Drive to Burns was fun and games.
An M.B. in Fog on snow and slush

Guess who from & where. Can you read it Dear. single penning no rewrite or corrections to this recollection. K.

with a tired driver perusing the Pas t.
Time was not so swift esp. after the
Snow plow drifts at less than 35 M.P.H
In Burns in good shape know Republic
will not make the trip but ready to go
if the flo[w] is so[-]so.
Transition is great-here ready to eat.
Ponderosa is the choice-1/2 liter of wine.
Believe it or not Chicken prunes to be
The pick of mine-and I eat every course
thinking back in time-It[']s been 12 wks.
since you and I were here life of mine.
Salut[´] to a fine time and hope a
replay of same will be mine. Love k-1-27-81.

<-> Check the newspaper for the events of the day. One Dead 2 on the way. Auto acc.[ident] up Bachelor way. Prom.[inent] citizen you had a hard day today. K.

This poem includes an addendum-more than one, in fact. First off, he writes a little note to Mom next to the title which is also the date he wrote the poem-[1-27-81]. The note reads- "Guess who from/& where./Can you read/it/Dear." Next to this little note is another at a slant that travels down the page-"single penning/no rewrite or/correction to/this/recollection/K. This is to let her know that instead of starting over with this rendering, he is simply going to produce his addendum which he places below the slanted note. He draws a double arrow [<->] to indicate where this addendum belongs in regard to the main body of the poem. I'll get to it as we read along.

It starts out -"Was an interesting day because/I got to stay-at the hospital/for a prolonged delay." (The hospital he speaks of is St. Charles in Bend, Oregon). He goes on-"It was only an inconvenience for me/ because all I had to do was stay…" He "got to stay" in line 2 versus his having to stay in line 5. Maybe the getting to stay alludes to the drama of the hospital atmosphere that day, and his having to stay is more about the inconvenience and tragedy of the scene. This is where the double arrows come in to the right of the main body of the poem. It reads-"Check the/newspaper/for the/ events of/ the day./One dead/2 on the way/auto acc./up Bachelor/way./Prom [inent]/citizen/you/had a hard/day/today./ K." So here he explains the reason he was detained at St. Charles-to tend to these victims-one the prominent citizen who he speaks directly to in the arrowed addendum-"You had a hard day today" as opposed to himself-"… all I had to do was stay [at St. Charles, longer than expected], not to mention that one in the accident was already "… dead/ [and] 2 on the/way [to their deaths]. So there were other victims, which dead, we don't know-the prominent citizen among the ones who didn't make it? I was aware, while growing up, that Dad's job was difficult. In this instance, he spends hours delayed from his travel to Eastern Oregon, where he will spend more time on the job. He was also such an emotional man, and instances such as the one he describes here, did him in. So he pens this note to her in order to share this experience with her on paper, in hopes that the sharing will ease his distress. Mom used to say that his job was too hard for him.

Dad mentions the patients he treated at the hospital on that day. He also tells Mom to check the newspaper for details. This was an exception to his rule, I believe only because it would be a news story. Otherwise, it is unlikely he would have said anything about these people, for he never talked about his patients to family or friends. However, sometimes one of us would discover something about someone in our community-and only then would Dad say he had known of that for a long time. Mom knew this about him and so did I.

Next, he continues on with a rendition of the remainder of his day, for he must now travel to Burns in Eastern Oregon for his work there-"Drive to Burns was fun and games/An M.B. (Mercedes-Benz) in fog on snow and slush/with a tired driver perusing the Pas t." He is the tired driver scrutinizing the pass and their past-a complicated drive. Here, again, he creates one word to make two-"Pas t" in line 8 is the pass and it ['] s a slow, tired and treacherous road, but is also his and her past that he ponders over. He describes this drive- "Time was not so swift (it dragged in fact)/esp. [especially] after the/snow plow drifts [along] at less than 35 M.P.H." Finally, he gets to his destination-"In Burns in good shape (as opposed to the car load of folks coming down from Mt. Bachelor)/know Republic will not make the trip but ready to go/ if the flow is so-so." I think here he refers to his medical associates as the "Republic." Republic is (#85, pg. 1236, 2. any group whose members are regarded as having a certain equality, common aims, etc.). He doesn't anticipate that anyone else from his clinic will make it over in the weather, but he will manage if the evening is slow with "the flow [of patients] so-so".

Finally, he goes out for his evening meal-"Transition is great-here ready to eat" and relax after a taxing day. He describes his evening out-"Ponderosa is the choice [he makes]-1/2 liter of wine/ Believe it or not chicken [pies?] to be/the pick of mine-and I eat every course/thinking back in time-It ['] s been 12 wks./since you and I were here [,] life of mine." As usual, while away, his thoughts drift back to her. He adds his endearing expression for her-Life of mine" because she was. He always returned to their times together when on his own, and this was no exception. He makes a salutation to the memory of their last visit to Burns together 12 weeks ago-Salute' to a fine time and hope a/replay of same will be mine."

[With] Love K-1-27-81
Pine Room [no date]
Solemn bored faces in the countryside
Hear names like Curly and Stud
Bulky guys [with] big boots and hats
Waitresses aged and homely but
fast on their feet
Believe it or not a gray [-] haired
lady passed gas on her way to the door
They file in at a steady pace.
Stays in general are quiet & short
what ['] s happened [to] that 30 yr. old
couple silently eating [,] not sharing
empty stares
Look around [and] you will see it all
Pine room drama [,] ceiling to floor.

The Pine Room was another of the few restaurants in Burns, Oregon that Dad frequented during his stays there. As in the previous poem, he visited the clinic or hospital for work and sometimes spent a night or two. In the early days of his career as a radiologist he and his partner took care of all such needs in Central- and Eastern Oregon-including Bend, Redmond, Prineville, Madras and Burns. On this night it was Burns and the Pine Room that he chose. He observes the atmosphere and clientele-"Solemn bored faces in the countryside/Hear names like Curly and Stud/Bulky guys [with] big boots and hats". Burns was and is Cowboy Country. Dad didn't really fit in but he seemed to get along with the folks there and developed an interest in wearing Cowboy gear as time went by. Initially, he had been a city slicker in Chicago. Maybe he thought wearing the local's type of clothing would help him fit in, I don't know. Anyway, that's what he did. Next he observes the waitresses there-"Waitresses aged and homely but/fast on their feet"-it seems he may have appreciated the good service these aged, homely women provided him. His next focus is-on the customers-"Believe it or not a gray haired/ lady passed gas on her way to the door"-again, it seems, he is amused by the manner of behavior in this part of the state. He elaborates on the clientele in the joint-"They file in at a steady pace./Stays in general are quiet & short/what ['] s happened [to] that 30 yr. old/couple silently eating [,] not sharing/empty stares" Dad was a keen observer of others, and, as I've mentioned earlier on, often made judgment by comparing others to himself and Mom-their relationship. He is astounded that a young couple would be so jaded while yet so young, comparatively speaking. I 'll have to admit that when I see couples looking bored with each other while out for a meal, I think to myself, why not just stay home? Dad ends tying up the poem with his final observation and estimation-"Look around you will see it all/ Pine room drama ceiling to floor. If it is drama he sees, it is surely dull drama. Is he being jocose?

A pen [K-4-81]

A fine simple point

A collection of ink above

Transferred by mind and hand
To an adore you for the
one I love in
script
That can be large or small
To convey miraculously
Any feeling mind to mind
a period of Tenderness
recorded for all time
To write with such a pen
Is extacy [ecstasy] for
It writes I love you so
delicately.
K-
4-81

In this poem Dad focuses on the power of the pen, and also the mechanics in the process of writing. He describes the tool of his trade-"A fine simple point"-He is careful with his cursive in this poem and makes small circles rather than dots above each letter "i" to accentuate his "fine simple point". In the first line, the circles even take on the appearance of a heart shape that I suspect was intentional. There are different meanings of the word point here, for he will make a "simple point" in the coarse of his writing. Some definitions of point are (#86, pg. 1129, 19. the exact essential fact or idea under consideration, 21. the important or main idea. 12. a sharp projecting end of something; hence, 13. something with a sharp end). So there is the point of the pen that lends itself to his ability to present his idea-the point or thought itself.

The second line-"a collection of ink above" is the pen's ink in its barrel above the point of the pen, that is "Transferred by [his] mind and hand/[in] To [his message] an [I] adore you [and is] for the/one I love in/script" Script is (#87, pg. 1311, 1. handwriting; words, letters, or figures. 3. a style of handwriting ;manner or method of forming letters or figures). This script "…can be large or small/ [and able] to convey miraculously/Any feeling mind to mind." Convey is to (#88, pg. 323, 3. communicate, make known, represent in words) and miraculously is (#89, pg. 939, 1.having the nature of a miracle; supernatural). The thought comes to mind and his hand transfers the thought to paper. Feelings are then shared "mind to mind", without spoken words, but instead, feelings conveyed from one mind to the other. And these words will be preserved, unlike spoken words that will dissolve from the moment.

In the next lines Dad elaborates-"A period of Tenderness/ recorded [on paper with pen] for all time"-that is, eternity. He then describes how this exercise influences him-"To write with such a pen/is ecstasy for/It writes I love you so/delicately". Here, the "so" can be interpreted as "I love you so [much] or the pen "writes [the] I love you [very] delicately". The way he writes with the pen- "delicately"-is cause for his delight because of the end product of his creation-the poem-the very beauty of his written cursive and the message it conveys-leads to his ecstasy. He emphasizes this feeling by copying his own written word-"delicately"-by tracing over it again. The pen is his vehicle (means) of his creation; the pen plays out his emotions for her-another example of his love's eternal quality.

Cheryl Krkoč

Burns #2 [5-5-82]   But can you read it.
I ordered a full carafe
for myself but found it
is enough for two or at least 1 ½ .
Ordered the T-bone not
chicken cuz [because] you weren't There.
Didn't notice [,] had the small.
But I must say-Big is
the way.
Found there was no big anyway.
then I have only one hint.
Cut next to the bone &
work your way out on
The N.Y. side. Leave the
rest for the dogs outside.
Made it early [,] Done by
7:30-Crowd not as
===== Sturdy-Waitress
still burly.
Looked over my shoulder
Was not sure But lo &
Behold [,] he didn't appear
Dear Bill
For dessert or even the
meal.
Plan to go to the tavern
For a beer and a cut
of the cards if it

will be.
Found one thing
For sure [,] Boyd ['] s
decaff [decaf] beats
Sanka forever and
a year.-Carry it
and order ==
Hot water my dear.
I only hope you
agree for I
love you – see.
Nevertheless in Burns it ['] s
The darndsst [darnedest] crowd we
Ever espy. 5.5.82
to [too] bad it was not 83
(Boyd ['] s is better [-] I will get you some
To carry

This rambling poem is a sequel of sorts to Pine Room or possibly 1-27-81 where Dad ate at the Ponderosa in Burns. He doesn't speak of the name of the restaurant he dines in here on 5-5-82, but the atmosphere and clientele sound like that which he described in the undated "Pine Room" poem.

This evening he writes-"I ordered a full carafe/for myself but found it/is enough for two or at least 1 ½" He tells her that there probably would have been enough for her if she had been there, and too much for him as it was. This poem is written with a combination of printed and cursive writing and what appears to be a rather shaky hand. This might explain why he adds a little note to Mom near the poem's title-"But can/you/read/it". Next, to go along with the carafe, he "ordered the T-Bone not/chicken cuz [because] you weren' T here."-apparently, the chicken dish was something they had shared together in the past. The "T" is capitalized and slanted towards the word "here" in small letters, in a way that the capital "T' can belong to the word weren't [you weren't here]. It also appears to read as "cuz [because] you weren't there, which lends itself to confusion about whether he is saying "you weren't here" or "you weren't there". I believe he meant both and intentionally wrote the line as such in order to allow for both meanings at once. The first suggests that he writes while in the restaurant and, in the second, his time frame is after he leaves and returns to his motel. Maybe he intended to include both because he thought of her before, during, and after his meal. It looks as though he wrote this poem on a paper place mat [with the foliage in the left margin of the second page]-again- before, during and/or after his meal.

In line 6 and 7-"Didn't notice [that I] had the small/but I must say-Big is/the way." Apparently, he was disappointed in the size of the steak, but in the next line-">Found out there was no big anyway." It turns out he actually had the one and only size offered, so he shares a hint for her, should she find herself ordering the T-Bone sometime in the future-"then I have only one hint/Cut next to the bone &/work your way out on/The N.Y. side." (He always was a meticulous type of eater too). Dad has had enough of this meal, because of the fact that he didn't get the non-existent large size and "leaves[s] only the bones for the dogs outside-"-there's the "N.Y. side" and then the "dogs outside". He "Made it

Love Poems and Obsession

early [and] done by/7:30-Crowd not as/== sturdy-[but] waitress/ still burly"-a reference to the type of waitresses he describes in the poem "Pine Room".

He may start to feel particularly lonesome for he tells her and/ or the reader-"Looked over my shoulder/was not sure But lo & behold he didn't appear". Maybe he had anticipated meeting his friend there-"Dear Bill/for dessert or even/the meal"-but that didn't happen and so he will "Plan to go to the tavern/for a beer and a cut/of the cards if it/will be." He never says whether or not he does this.

Finally, back at the motel, his focus goes in the direction of a find-"Found one thing/for sure Boyd ['] s /decaf beats/Sanka forever and/a year." And guess what-you can "carry it and order/ Hot water [in the room] my dear." Dad could always be entertained and delighted by the simplest things-in this case, Boyd's decaf and hot water for it in his room and he writes to let her know all about it. He writes-"I only hope you/agree for I/love you-see." He anticipates a future in sharing the adventure of Boyd's decaf with her because he loves her-"[you] see". He ends with his last observation that he wants to share with her-"Nevertheless in Burns its/ the darnedest crowd we/ever espy"-for it seems that they have shared this observation of the crowd sometime in the past while in Burns. He signs off with his signature "K " in the midst of his final refrain, and adds the date below-5.5.82-along with another comment in writing-"to [too] bad it was not [19]83"-and would that mean she might be with him? And finally, a promise-"Boyd['] s/is better [so] I will get you some/to carry [with you]".

Cheryl Krkoč

Post Script-Dad always collected items in restaurants, hotel or motel rooms, lobbies, taverns and bars for future use or for sentimental reasons. He delighted in these types of sundries and would dole them out to family members on a regular basis. I suspect his growing up years during the Great Depression had something to do with this hobby of his, but I also think it had to do with his sentimental nature.

> *Feb. 83 [2-1-83]*
> *Sitting in Burns you see*
> *Watching the crowd*
> *In a new Outpost*
> *Pine Room was closed.*
> *Chicken was greasy beer Desert & coffee too.*
> *But only 9.96 [with] salad &wine-*
> *Plate was cold.*
> *Butter was Oleo and*
> *The service was slow.*
> *Guess what I did [,] read*
> *the paper*
> *also*
> *thought of L.A. [with] Sweet you.*
> *Then-Don't know why.*
> *Slipped to Bud McCusker*
> *He still works you see*
> *Hoblingly [Hohhlingly]*
> *They mention [Dr.] White but*
> *never Bud-So Sad.*
> *I hope when we go*

Love Poems and Obsession

> *Someone-anyone will say K-2-1-83*
> *eather [either] of the K's are going away*

Here we have another poem written while Dad is in Burns. It is February 1st of 1983-several months after the last poem was written-"Burns #2". He always seems full of contemplation when away from home and especially while alone. He starts out-"Sitting in Burns you see/watching the crowd/In a new Outpost/Pine Room was closed"-so now he has found another god-forsaken spot for a meal. Everywhere in Burns can be referred to as an outpost, for it's in the middle of nowhere. Maybe this makes Dad's stays there even more lonely and contemplative and so he does what he usually does when dining alone-he is "watching the crowd". He describes this meal in an uncomplimentary manner-"Chicken was greasy/Plate was cold."Then, he interjects a line between these two lines that travels up the page in the right-hand margin-"But only 9.96 [with] salad & wine-Beer Desert & Coffee too." He continues on with complaints-Butter was Oleo [his pet- peeve] and/The service was slow [a less annoying peeve]."

Dad frequently argued with wait staff about what was presented as butter but, in his estimation, wasn't. He would even go so far as to demonstrate his point by either asking the attendant to melt it, or he himself would manage the task, which, he would insist, could prove his point. The butter, he would explain, would retain some milky residue, while the fraudulent substance, such as Oleo, would not. All this was a great humiliation, for those of us at the table with him, to bear. It seems, though, that on this particular night, and while dining alone, he didn't get into it with anyone.

Dad changes the subject in the next few lines-"Guess what I did [?] read/the newspaper/also/ thought of L.A. with Sweet you." He goes back to his favorite solitary pastimes-reading the paper, daydreaming about Jean, this time memories of their time in L.A. together. He changes focus again-"Then-don't know why/skipped to Bud McCusker/He still works you see/Hobblingly/They mention "… White but/never Bud. So Sad"- Bud was a good doctor friend of Dad's for many years, a little older than he. Dad sees him starting to fail-He works "hobblingly" The other doctors mention and pay attention to White-an assumingly younger, more proficient physician, while ignoring Bud. Dad sees his own future in Bud, his friend and colleague, and all these thoughts wander to the next related topic-"I hope when we go/someone-anyone will [notice and] say/eather [either] of the K's are going away"

He hopes "Someone-Anyone" will pay attention to their passing on. Dad spells the word "eather", not either. I suspect this was intentional in order to provide the word with more than one meaning as he often did. Ether (or aether) is (#90, pg. 498, 2. the upper region of space) and the related ethereal is (#91, pg. 499, 3. heavenly; celestial; not earthly). This word can also be a substitute for the word either. Two definitions of either are (#92, pg. 464, 1. one or the other (of two) and 2. each (of two); the one and the other). So I believe Dad is using both of the two definitions-he is saying that both of them will be leaving the earth behind, hopefully, together, and to an ethereal celestial forever together. However, he also hopes that "someone-anyone" will notice their departure and then absence, and we did. However, they didn't leave at the same time as Dad always hoped. That's why, in their later years, they flew from place to place, with his hope that on one of these flights, the plane would go down. It just didn't happen that way though. He signs off on the right-hand margin-traveling up the page-K-2-1-83. He was 56 when he wrote this poem and would have another 29 years left on earth-not all so good.

Sweet Trip [12-19-83]
Back in Time
Old movie sent via waves
Hawaii local. Fifties scene
Purity patriotism and J. Wayne
but only
Small background fragments
Jarred my memory and
I swam into a
nostalgic extacy [ecstasy].
My mind engaged in
Fleeting moments of sublime
Pleasure.
Had you been there
Those floating sweet Lay Lonnie
Strains shared in silence would
Have been sweeter at the time.
But sharing with a written page
Also has its place I feel.
Love K 12-19-83

This poem is about imagination and how the mind works. It comes disjointed, fragmented, vivid, and fantastical. It can set all the senses afire. It's like a dream, or more than real. It travels forwards and backwards, turns into a jumble, sets the soul into outer-space, can make us weep or laugh out-loud, makes us remember, imagine the future or leave time behind altogether.

Dad goes "Back in Time" in this poem-His mind is [like an] "Old movie sent via [by way of] waves/Hawaii local."

Next, his mind goes to a "Fifties scene/Purity patriotism and J. Wayne"-all trademarks of his generation. He elaborates on his musings-"but only/Small background fragments" emerge in his mind and "Jarred my memory." His mind settles on vague fragments of though which somehow lead to jarring his memory in a new direction-"I swam into a nostalgic ecstasy"-a memory of an Hawaiian ocean swim-Nostalgia is (#93, pg. 1003, 2. a longing for something far away or long ago) and ecstasy is (#94, pg. 459, 1. a state of being overpowered with emotion, especially joy). His "…mind engaged in/Fleeting moments of sublime/Pleasure" which gives the impression of a dream-like but also realistic state of being in the Hawaiian ocean water again. His state of mind brings on this physical "sublime" and sensual quality.

In line 13 there's a shift. He comes out of his day dream-"Had you been there [he says to her]/Those floating sweet Lay Lonnie/Strains shared in silence would/Have been sweeter at the time." He lets her know that "had [she] been there" in his daydream, somehow she would have entered into his fantasy in a real sense, and also would have heard, as he did, "Those floating sweet Lay Lonnie/Strains"-the melodic tropical songs "floating" through the breeze" and, if shared "would have been sweeter" than his solitary musings had been. However, they would have been shared in silence, for each would have had their own version playing inside their heads-strains of music they had shared in the past. But since she wasn't there to share his fantasy, Dad writes-"But sharing with a written page/also has its place I feel." When he is alone, without her, the only way he is able to share his experience is to share "with a written page"-at least he shares it all with the page, as if the page is hearing what he has found in his fantasy, and then there becomes a record for himself and to share with others who might read it later, in particular, Mom.

March 30, '83 Unpolished
Sat in the Pine Room
without you
Thought to myself-
Thirty plus years of quest
Gave
An arrowhead collection
To two
Equal in some odd way as
I see thee and me
So with deep respect and
a degree of awe
I will buy If I can
This symbolic memento
of the life they knew.
And dedicate it to you
So we can reflect
with due respect
What will be left
of us
Oh museum poor lost idea

Now you are to be
a symbolic memento.
May be Later K-83

As mentioned, Dad would frequent the Pine Room often while in Burns, Oregon for work, as is apparent by how often the place is a subject in his poetry. Maybe the desolate nature of Eastern Oregon intensified his bent towards melancholy and loneliness while there. In this poem, it is the old couple that own and operate the place that is the focus here. He starts out-"Sat in the Pine Room/without you/thought to myself-/Thirty plus years of quest/Gave/ An arrow head collection/To/two" The old couple spent years out in the desert running their tavern and collecting arrowheads on their days off. They had them framed and displayed over the bar for many years. It turned out, I believe, that there got to be thirteen large black-framed collections in all. Dad had admired them for years and, in fact, had made many offers to purchase them, but the old couple held out. For one thing, they had sentimental attachment of their own, and for the other, it enhanced the character of their place.

The next lines-"Equal in some odd way as/I see thee and me". He sees the old couple and their collection as a reflection of himself and his beloved-their own lives together-a unique quest of its own. (He truly obsessed about all this and all of us kids heard about the couple and the collection for years.) Next, he writes about what he plans to do-"So with deep respect and/a degree of awe/I will buy If I can/This symbolic memento/of the life they knew/and dedicate it to you". A memento is (#95, pg. 917, 1. in the Roman Catholic Church, either of two prayers in the Canon of the Mass, one for the living and one for the dead, Beginning "Memento"). A "memento mori" is in (#96, pg. 917, [Latin, remember that you must die], any reminder of death). The symbolic memento here is the collection the couple created together. It also seems that the remnants of the indigenous Native People-the arrow heads-speak to those whose artifacts still exist, but who have gone to another place.

It was only after the old guy died that his widow finally agreed to sell the collection to Dad, maybe in hopes that he would carry on the torch-a memento mori, at least while he could. Dad's hope is "So we can reflect/with due respect/what will be left of us". He hopes the collection will be a reminder of the significance of both relationships, and then when they too are gone, the symbol will remain.

After Dad acquired the collection he made an attempt to donate it to a local museum, but he was told that the intention was to disassemble each of the thirteen black-framed beauties and rework them for exhibition. But Dad refused these terms because he had promised the widow they would remain intact while in his care-preserving the couple's creations of the desert. Thus, there is the line-"Oh museum poor lost idea/Now you are to be/a symbolic memento./May be later". His intention, it seems, had been to share the pieces for the museum and its guests to appreciate, but now the failed museum idea becomes a "memento more"-a reminder of death. However, his line-"May be later" offers the promise of eternal love, and to preserve each couple's significance, and symbolic immortality through the collection.

What Dad decided to do was to split the collection amongst his four children and his grandchildren have an eye on the pieces, so maybe his plan will prevail. Post script-He added an underlined "unpolished" at the top right margin that slants down the page. I wonder what he thought was amiss. But I think his poetry was his arrowhead collection-"What will be left of us [?]"-One thing-maybe his poetry.

Sweet Thing [10-17-83]
Down tonight-Hope the A.M. is Bright.
Rockeffeler [Rockefeller] Square - Lots of flowers there.
One less God Bless stay fresh.
Tonight - Sampled the street and
things to eat.
But no big discovery my sweet.
One place I hit. Prodori
oven. Tried for the Bread
But don't know yet. Will
I get the dough. But I
Will let you know.
Remember one thing. You never
Spoil anything only make it
Supreme or if not well a little less
so. K- 10-17-83

This poem begins with "Down tonight". Dad had his predisposition to melancholy, as I've mentioned before. He hopes the morning will be better-"Hope the A.M. is Bright". He must have been in N.Y.C. when he wrote this poem for he mentions Rockefeller Square, although he spells it Rockeffeler-"Rockeffeler

Love Poems and Obsession

Square-Lots of flowers there"-so he picks one for her-"One less [flower] God Bless [,] stay fresh-He asks God to keep the flower in good condition until he returns home with the one picked flower for her. Next, he wanders about-"Tonight-Sampled the street and/things to eat/But no big discovery my sweet." He seems rather bored without her there. But then he tells of the Prod.Ori Oven-"He "tried for the bread/But don't know yet. Will/I get the dough. But I/will let you know." I'm not sure what he means here, but maybe he intended to have some bread or dough shipped back home and is unsure if he can make this happen. At any rate, he plans to let her know how it all turns out. In general, so far in this poem, he describes lackluster as he wanders about New York City-a place he usually raved about. Something or someone was missing.

In the last three lines he abandons his discussion about his aimless wandering and writes more intimately to her-"Remember one thing [.] You never/Spoil anything only make it/supreme [,] or if not [,] well a little less so." He hopes to reassure her about how she has a positive effect on him, but then, qualifies this declaration with the last phrase-"…or if not [,] well a little less so". It seems he is admitting that sometimes she misses the mark in making their time together as good as it could be, but at least she "never/spoil [s] anything". This was said in his "down" mood, mentioned in the first line, when nothing much seemed to interest him at all. Post script. I note smudge marks on his cursive for the words Prod.Ori, and in the following line, the word "the" underneath the beginning of Prod.Ori. There are also smudges further down in the last two lines, of the words "only", "make" and "little". I wonder if the smudged letters are the result of tears shed while he penned this one-were they tears of joy or sadness?

Jean [1984]
In a moment of tender time
Our fingers may entwine
Form a knot of love
Eyes shine be mine
Gentle squeeze a
Cheek kiss-Brush
a tress of hair
It's all there
Love
Bob
84

This poem, I will title Jean, is encased by a heart. He starts out-"In a moment of tender time/Our fingers may entwine/Form a knot of love". He provides a visual for the reader of their mutual devotion. Next he makes an entreaty-"Eyes shine be mine" and then describes his signs of his affection for her- "Gentle squeeze a/Cheek kiss-Brush/a tress of hair", and finally, he summarizes all these gestures-"It's all there." And as a love letter would end, he signs "Love/Bob/84".

Harry's Bar [1-25-84]
I sat alone [,] shed a tear
You were not there.
Amarone 14% too much
alone.
Crowd not quite the same

Love Poems and Obsession

Like us
a parody
Gee
I asked why-Oh See
No theatre
oh me
I suspect. May I
May we be an
oddity-
No-May wee
Last night was
"sh___" you see.
Love thee.
Lonely K
Harry's Bar
1-25-84
[left margin] "9:30-Brandy in The Plaza Bar [with] Cigar then to bed by 6 a.m.
[right margin] "Set it up [with] Alexander and Craig. Montecelloe [Monticello] for 2
Table 3: [f]or 2-Sat [urday] 7 cocktails then Dinner at 8:00. Can [no] t wait.

Harry's Bar at Century City in Los Angeles is where Dad's Slovenian buddy Bruno was a waiter. He always showed Mom and Dad and our family a good time. This time, though, Dad seems to have been alone. It also seems he penned this poem after his meal there. He starts out-"I sat alone shed a tear/ [because] you were not there". He ordered the Amarone-a rich

Italian dry red wine-that they likely shared in the past, but it was "14% too much/alone". It makes me wonder if he was lit while writing this one, as the content seems a little vague.

As he has suggested in other of his poems, he writes that the "crowd not quite the same/Like us/a parody/Gee". He judges the crowd as not measuring up to them. A parody is (#97, pg. 1064, 2. a poor or weak imitation) so that is what he thinks of those in the crowd. He asked why-then See ['s the light]-There is no "theatre" or drama when they are not somewhere together, he decides with an exclamation-"oh me [oh my]".

Next, he writes "I suspect. May I/May we be an/oddity-No may wee". He seems to answer the question he asks himself. I'm not sure where he is going with this but he asks-"…May I/May we be an/oddity", but answers "No-May wee". He asks the question "may we" and then asks again "May wee". Is it that they are unique in his mind only as a unit-"Wee"-the two ee's a sign of unity? Or can wee also mean "a little bit" of an oddity? Or is he making no sense at all because of the bottle of "Amerone14%"-too/much to drink all by himself-known to have a higher that average (14%) alcohol level. Finally, in the last three lines of the main body of the poem, he tells her that "Last night was/sh[it] you see"-for she was not there to share the evening with him.

Dad added two side-bars that ran along either side of the main body of the poem. On the left he writes-"9:30-Brandy in the Plaza Bar [with] Cigar then to bed by 6 a.m." Did he stay up all night? On the right margin he writes-"Set it up [with] Alexander & Craig.-Montecelloc [Monticello Hotel in Los Angeles] for 2/Table 3: [f]or 2-Sat. 7 coctails [cocktails] then Dinner at 8:00. [I] Can [no] t wait." I suspect he made arrangements for them to have an extravagant evening In Los Angeles. She would fly down to meet him after his conference was over, and he was eager for this sweet reunion-"Cant wait".

Jean [2-23-85]
Bar's a lonly [lonely] place
Solitude
Cigar fills the space
Smoke spirals into the air
Carries a dream
Oh smoke ring
etherial [ethereal] thing
you Bring
Back the memory of
A prior place
Sweet thing you
Hold an everlasting place
K-2-23-85 No more space.

Here again Dad finds himself alone in a bar, pining away for his mate. He describes his surroundings as "a lonely place/[in]Solitude". He often writes about smoke rings coming from his cigar. It seems his observation of them takes him to the mystical place-"Solitude". The cigar smoke "…fills the space/ [as the] smoke spirals in to the air/[and] carries a dream"-his dream. He enters into an alternate reality-a dream made real-"an ethereal thing". As mentioned, the word ethereal is (#98, pg. 499, 3. heavenly; celestial; not earthly), and he addresses this magic in a personal way, as if speaking to a divine thing-"You Bring/Back the memory of/a prior place". He transcends worldly limitations. Transcends is (#99, pg. 1546, 3. separate from or beyond experience, the material universe, etc.) Then, I believe, in the next two lines-"Sweet thing you/Hold an everlasting place"-he speaks directly to his wife and tells her that this transcendent state of his will hold her in an everlasting place in his soul. He has one last line-"No more space"-on his scrap of paper that seems to have been cut from a larger lined notebook page. He wants to let her know that if there had been more room to write additional thoughts on the matter, he would have. He signs off K-2-23-85.

I Love Jean [no date]
I love Jean [and] she makes
me go out of my bean as you
have seen. Cheer up the
chicken soup is good for body
and soul. And it will be blessed Bobby

In this five-line poem Dad starts out with a proclamation (to himself and potential readers) about his feelings for his wife. He is so exuberant about her that he writes that he loves her and that "she makes/me go out of my bean"… Bean is (#100, pg. 128, 6. [Slang], head; brain; mind) and so going out of his mind is what happens when she is around. He adds …"as you/have seen"-addressing his audience-anyone who might read this ditty and/or who is familiar with their relationship, and especially others in the household who have seen and are aware of her effect on him-hence, the 'you' in "as you have seen"-obvious to all.

Love Poems and Obsession

In the next two and a half lines Dad addresses her directly-"Cheer up the/chicken soup is good for body/and soul, and it will be blessed" Mom always worried about the outcome of whatever came out of her kitchen, so he tries to reassure her here-"And it will be blessed"-blessed-almost a holy thing for all those who partake of her nourishing meal and perhaps a form of Holy Communion.

Paper and Me [8-20-85]

Hour & 45

Missed you [,] no Steak

Where were you tonight

Had a nice flight.

Shrimp

Brown Bread and

Bean Soup

Oh Fried chicken

Tomorrow I'll poop

Ice creame [cream] and

Coffee-

Finee [Fini]-

Oh Gee

No cigar you See

Love thee K-

8-20-85

Your are part of my life

Long heart

tonight.

I noticed that this poem seems to have been written on a paper place mat that was cut in the shape of a heart at some point. It also appears to have a raised uniform pattern along the periphery of the poem. At first I thought this might be a series of water stains left during Dad's meal, but with further inspection of the original poem, I suspect the cause may be glue used to secure the poem to the album. It may have been the nature of this type of paper that caused the rather unique, intimate and three-dimensional pattern attached to this particular poem.

Dad titles this poem "Paper and Me"-indicative of his relationship with pen and paper. He always preferred the fountain pen and ink bottle sort of writing material and he used this method until it became more difficult to find such instruments for writing. I remember as a child how he would dip the pen's point delicately into the ink bottle, giving him time to formulate and write his next thought and then he would start all over again. I was fascinated with his manner of writing-so much more romantic and creative than with a modern pen, or even worse, with a computer. This particular poem was written with a ball point, and so, doesn't portray his distinctive cursive as others he wrote with his original method. Anyway, back to the poem.

Here again, he is on his own with work or business, having a solitary meal. The meal and/or his flight lasts an "hour & 45 [minutes]" and then "Missed you [,] no Steak/Where were you tonight" [?] He complains about not having a steak as a part of his meal and casually adds the question of where she might have been when he tried to call her. Is he suspicious of her? He moves on to a more detailed description of his evening and meal-"Had a nice flight/Shrimp/ Brown Bread and/Bean Soup/Oh [and also] Fried Chicken" and this large meal will surely mean that "Tomorrow I'll poop". But that's not all. Now he describes more of it-"Ice cream and/coffee-/Fini-/ [but] Oh Gee/No cigar you See"-Coffee, Fini, and Gee all rhyme. Somehow the meal is not complete without his after dinner cigar. But he recovers from this disappointment enough to tell her that he loves her-"Love thee" and adds "You are part of my life", and finally, he wants her to know that without her with him, he has a "Long heart/tonight." P.S. Fini is French for finished.

I reply [9-5-85]

Note: Mom sent a Western Union telegram to Dad from Los Angeles, California on 9/3/1985 from The Century Plaza Hotel. I was down there with Mom, who had arranged for us to go there together. On the way, there was an earthquake that left us in the air circling until the quake subsided. We also had aftershocks that night at exactly 4:00 a.m.-the high rise hotel waving and then pounding violently. Mom never did wake up but ran to the windows where pool inhabitants scurried out of the pool. A sight to see! Anyway, the message's entirety from Mom was "Love You. Jean". This was one of the only times I was aware of her expressing verbal sentiment in writing towards Dad. He responded to her message with the poem, I Reply. My commentary follows.

I reply
Implicitly
Simplicity is best
To express
The mind ['] s sublime
If done on Time
Here are

Frank [']s
Thanks
L. you 2
9-5-85

He starts out–"I reply/Implicitly". Implicit can be (#101, pg. 730, 2. suggested or to be understood though not plainly expressed; implied, or 4. without reservation or doubt; unquestioning; absolute). It seems he is suggesting that both of them already know of this love between them even if it isn't mentioned. Next he writes "Simplicity is best/To express/ The mind's sublime/ If done on Time". I believe here he compliments her on her simple message of "Love you" which says it all. Maybe it was sent at just the right time, when he was feeling lonely-hence-"...sublime/if done on Time". Time is capitalized-the right time, or maybe even Timeless. In the next few lines he thanks her and sends a similar simple message back with "L. you 2".

Day By Day [11-15-85]
Mind chronicles your faraway stay
Still feel I love your every way
Wondering what we will first say
On the comming [coming] November Sunday
Not much but
My mind and heart will glow that day
Then after you recover from the lag
To toast after the long delay
with a chosen burgundy Romane'e
Or possibly as you wish
The one fourteen will be the dish

Then hopefully Together we shall lay
In heavenly foreplay.
I pray
Day by Day
K
11-15-85

Dad was usually the one away from home. He always missed Mom as is apparent in many of his poems that address this topic. After Mom was a little older, though, and we kids were gone or not in need of as much attention from her, she took up traveling on her own or with one of us kids. I know she took two trips to Israel, one with a Roman Catholic group and another with the group and my sister Sandra. She also traveled back to Chicago to visit relatives without Dad at times. I'm not sure which trip Dad speaks of here but it seems more likely it was an extended stay, so likely one of her trips to Israel. It is apparent in this poem that Dad missed her as much when she was away from home as when he was. There isn't much evidence about her feelings in these matters because she never wrote much down, as far as I know, but Dad may have sent this poem to her while she was abroad.

Dad starts out this poem-"[My] Mind chronicles your faraway stay". He imagines where she is and what her experience is-maybe so that he can share in her travel and find joy for her in her adventure. His mind moves on to his sentimental feelings for her-"Still feel I love your every way"-he basks in his adoration of her. Next, he is "Wondering what we will first say/on the coming November Sunday"-now he looks forward to her return and imagines what it will be like, what they will say to each other, and, in general, what their reunion will be. In the fifth line he goes back to his question about what they might say to each other, and speculates that it will "Not [be] much but/ [that his] mind and heart will glow that day". I wonder about disappointment on his part, imagining that she won't share her adventure or say that she missed him. He speaks directly to her in this poem–"My mind and heart will glow that day"–no matter what condition she is in, and "then after you recover from the [jet] lag", they will celebrate, so maybe he just anticipates her need to recover after such a long journey. This celebration will include a bottle of Burgundy Romanee from what is considered the greatest wine producer in the world. He also mentions "the one fourteen" that will either accompany the Romanee or replace it–"as you wish", he tells her. Is he referring to "the dish" that might accompany the wine, or will the dish be another elixir? But all his daydreams and planning, he hopes, will culminate in romance–"Then hopefully together we shall lay/In heavenly foreplay". Finally, he prays his dreams will come true and this goes on "Day by Day" until her return.

The first time Dad visited Slovenija, Croatia and Italy was about the time he retired. His sister Jean talked him into going and I was invited too. We visited family there and after this first visit of his, he returned several times. I think his trips there led to his appreciation of his ethnicity and culture. As an immigrant's son, he certainly had a different perception of himself before the trips he and his family made because of dicrimination he suffered. He had asked Mom to go there with him after his first visit but she declined. In this letter he received from her while he was overseas, she expresses dismay over his absence. His letter to her, it seems, was meant to assuage her distress and confirm his devotion.

Dad's letter to Mom while he was in Slovenija: [7-16-94]
Dearest Jean:
I now know the month will be much
harder for you than me. But the degree
was a complete surprise to me. It
Must be because the children are no
Longer home since when we were young
During the course of a year we spent
Less time together than we do now–
Probably 2-3x more/yr. Even with all
my recent and present separations.
My 2 calls on the 15th probably hurt
more than they helped. I will try to
write cards while I am in Europe
as often as possible. It is not
a war [,] I am not in the service and
the time will go more quickly than
you imagine.
Hope you can read my small
writing.
Our bond is firm and good
We are lucky but please take
Some joy in my trip like I
Take joy from your visits with
Norbert.
With Sweet Sorrow

> *Love, Bobby*
> It seems both of them had difficulty with being separated!
> *See Love Stories [no date]*
> *See love stories on T-V*
> *Read Shakespeare Holmes Whitman and Thoreau*
> *Feel the essence of Romeo & Juliet etc.*
> *Vicarious projections abound but none are any more profound than those I have found*

Dad was a true romantic. Here he reports his familiarity with the topic of love and romance-"See love stories on T-V/Read Shakespeare Holmes Whitman and Thoreau/ [I] feel the essence of Romeo & Juliet etc." There was a true similarity between the story of the star-crossed lovers Romeo and Juliet and my parents for both couples had difficulty in regard to parental disapproval. In Mom and Dad's case, Mom's side of the family strongly objected to the union due to his immigrant family and religious differences. Their fate was not the same as Romeo and Juliet's but, nevertheless, problematic, resulting in Mom's ongoing emotional tumult. This is why, I believe, he writes part of the next line-"Vicarious projections abound…" Vicarious is (#102, pg. 1624, 1. taking the place of another person. 4. experienced by someone through his imagined participation in another's experience). Projection can mean-pg. 460.5a a mental image viewed as objective reality (ACD) Dad partakes of all these writers' works (in particular, the story of Romeo and Juliet) and takes the place of Romeo or other of the male characters in his imagination. He assigns the female characters to his real-life mate-hence, his "Vicarious projections". Finally, he proclaims that "…none/are any more profound than/ those I have found". His love is as significant and powerful as any he has come across.

Flames [12-21-85]
Like fires warmth and beauty
you still fill my eyes
Reflect.
Starts with much ado-a flicker
with some smoke then
slowly
Bursting into rising flames
that
spread at an ever increasing
pace
then
Slowly by embers to be replaced.
Transformed to an orange red sea
then to slowly fade away
Like silent aging
[I] experienced the fuss smoke and ado.
Have felt the motion the flame
the flow of love
and now [,]
like the embers inside [,] I still glow."
K-12-21-85
1st Day of Winter

Mom and Dad loved sitting in front of a fire. There were three fire-places in the home we occupied in Oregon during the time we kids were still home and for a while longer. But there was a fire-place in our first home in Chicago too. Dad always seemed mesmerized by the beauty of the flames and in this poem he likens the fire-place to life's ardor and to the passing of time-life's stages. First, he likens the fire's warmth and beauty to his lover-"Like fire [']s warmth and beauty/you still fill my eyes/Reflect." The scene is reminiscent of his lover's beauty and warmth and takes him to a meditative state of mind.

Next, he transitions to the evolution of the fire itself-"[it] starts with much ado [,] a flicker/with some smoke then/slowly/Bursting into rising flames/that/spread at an ever increasing/pace". I wonder if the "flicker" is the conception of life itself, and the subsequent "spreading at an ever increasing/pace" is the subject of the miracle of the developing fetus in the womb and life beyond the womb. After all this there is another reality-"Slowly by embers to be replaced". He reminisces here about his prior self, with all its vigor and passion. Now he is left, in his waning years with what he likens to "only embers" of what his life had been. He continues on with his description of the life cycle of fire and the human condition-[the embers are] "Transformed to an orange red sea/then to slowly fade away/Like silent aging" with the end result of death. The transformation, though, seems to have a beauty all its own. The embers are not showy like the roaring fire, but, in some respect, are even more beautiful. There is a tranquil quality to his musings. Finally, he makes a review of his life so far-"Experienced the fuss smoke and ado/Have felt the motion the flame/the flow of love". He has experienced, in his own mind, all that life has to offer "and now/like the embers inside, I still/glow". He has entered into the reminiscent faze of life, without, as yet, serious attention to the inevitable. He signs and dates the poem-"K-12-21-85/1st Day of Winter"-the first day of his winter.

Dad always seemed to have a keen sense of the life cycle from an early age, but also a spiritual sense that went along with it. Perhaps all this lies in his genetic makeup. Slovenians can be traced back to very ancient times. The Veneti, cousins to Etruscans, inhabited what is still Slovenija, but also the Italian peninsula, including what is now Sicily. There is also a connection to the Vinca Culture- the ancient civilized community in what is now South Eastern Europe and the Southern Balkans. Their language and culture was earthy, sensual, and spiritual, as evidenced by ancient relics from far back in time.

Wish for Jean [5-18-86]
Oh Morpheus sweet
spirit what secret
calls do you answer
Reveal your ways
To peaceful rest I pray
Calm spirit [,] fill my nights
[with] Rest
Let loose my tensions
of the mind
Relax my muscles in
short time-
Wake me rested & Pure.

To face the day so sure K-5-18-86

Dad was probably the only person on earth who came close to understanding Mom and her demons. Her anguish spilled out to all around her, and especially to Dad. In the first four words-"Oh Morpheus sweet/spirit"-Morpheus was the Greek god of dreams in Ovid's Metamorphoses. He had the ability to mimic any human form and to appear in dreams. His true semblance is that of a winged daemon. Anatomy of Melancholy refers to Classical depictions of Morpheus [that] signify good and bad (#104). Dad's reference to Morpheus seems to be that of Mom's subconscious torment. He pleads with her to find a way to peace, which, in turn, will free him as well, for his own concern for her well-being creates his own torment. First, he directly addresses her in the first four words-"Oh Morpheus sweet/spirit..."- and asks "what secret/calls do you answer" [?] Does this question of his suggest suspicion of an affair on her part? Are there phone calls she had that are unaccounted for? Or does this question more generally address her quiet, secret emotional state, a monologue that plays repeatedly inside her head? In the next line he seems to implore her to open up to him-"Reveal your ways" and if she does, this will allow him (and her) "...peaceful rest". He addresses himself and/or her as a transformed "Calm spirit" and hopefully anticipates "...nights/ [with] Rest [,]"Let[ting] loose [his and/or her] tensions of the mind/Relax[ing] of muscles in/short time-" if she will unburden herself to him. If all this happens, then they will both "Wake... rested & Pure/To face the day so sure" Unfortunately, if she did confide in him, it didn't seem to do much to allay her funk. It was only after she lost her mind to dementia that she was able to "forget" whatever it was that troubled her so and by that time it may have been too late for Dad to forget.

Stupidity [K-6-5-86]
More than two Hours late
For our anticipated date
Nicest thing I can emulate
Our meeting at the estate
What should I do
When my eyes perceive you
I old fool
Outward expression dull
Emotion null
Inside not true
The eight of you
That simple view
Content
With internal chaos
Transpires
So
Stupidly take refuge in the mail
Such Assininity [Asininity]
Forgive the complacency
With its utter stupidity
Love isn't absent-minded
 enmity or at
 least it should not be
K-6-5-86

This poem was written on my sister Nora's nineteenth birthday. It seems Dad was late getting home for the birthday celebration. He starts out-"More than two hours late/for our anticipated date". He was likely miles away, working in Eastern Oregon as he often did, before he was able to get home. So he returns home with the party in full force. Then-"Nicest thing I can emulate/Our meeting at the estate". I think he says he is trying to keep up with the revelry occurring at the already in-progress birthday party. What comes to mind is a previous "meeting at the estate" when he was in a different mood. He silently asks himself-"What should I do/when my eyes perceive you"-How should he purport himself, while in his rather foul mood, when he is supposed to feel differently? Then he describes himself as an "old fool" for having his outward dull expression and his null emotion during these festivities. He continues to defame himself-" (his)Inside not True (good)" and in contrast he sees "the eight of you/That simple view/ content". Now he will focus on his own comportment-"with internal chaos/Transpires/So/stupidly take refuge in the mail/Such asininity". His "internal chaos" leads him to retreat into perusal of the mail, and then, upon reflection, deems himself to be asinine. He continues to beat himself up over his perceived ruination of the party's mood due his own. Then he attempts to make amends to the others-"Forgive the complacency (#105, pg.298, 2. self satisfaction, smugness)/with its utter stupidity" and adds his emerging insight that-"Love isn't absent-minded/enmity (hostility) or at/least it should not be"

Along the right-hand margin of this poem he spells the word TURBULANCE in capital letters that run up the page. I think it sums up his internal state on returning home from a hectic day, two hours late, to find a birthday celebration in progress-I believe an understandable reaction under the circumstances. I do think he was too hard on himself. His job was demanding and sometimes Mom would tell me that it was too hard on him. He did enjoy his profession as a physician but it did take a toll.

In Less Than a Day [no date]
Motored over the pass
Through snow up to my [ass]
Arrived wind howling
And some downpour
Rain hail-felt pale-Then
Nestled in after
fish and chips
Lolled away the rest of the day
Evening walk-Small talk
Dinner at pier 101
Watching it snow
Then like magic
Wouldn't you know
Winds cease to blow
Clouds go
And in the cool still night
The stars shown bright
Some sight.

In this poem Dad tells of his partial day traveling to and then settling into the little coast town of Lincoln City. The first two lines suggest it was winter-"Motored over the pass/Through snow up to my [ass]". He leaves out the word ass that would have rhymed with "pass", I suppose to avoid using a rather raunchy word in his poem, but the message remains clear. The weather on this trip over is horrific-"Arrived the wind howling/And some downpour/Rain hail-felt pale". It seems the drive left him tense, hence, the word "pale" to describe his color. Finally, they get there. It is difficult, in the first part of the poem, to tell if he is traveling alone or not, but it becomes apparent that he has company. He describes that he or they "Nestled in after/fish and chips [for lunch]/Lolled away the rest of the day" and finally, the give-away, had an "Evening walk-[and] Small talk"-most likely with someone, unless he was talking to himself-not entirely out of the realm of possibility. Next, they had dinner at Pier 101 "Watching it snow". I remember Dad waxing poetic about the few weekends at the Oregon coast when they witnessed snow on the beach-a special time for Mom and Dad. It seems this was one of those times. However, the price for this treat was the treacherous drive over the pass that he describes to get there, and I do remember some of them myself. I never was lucky enough to see the snow covered beach for myself though.

The mood of the poem changes in the next line-"Then like magic/Wouldn't you know/Winds cease to blow/Clouds go". The weather has changed for the better-the dramatic rapid changes that are usual on the Oregon coast. You never know what you'll get from one day to the next, or even one hour to the next and this coastal weather changed much like Dad's moods. Finally, the epitome of the day seems to come after sundown-"And in the cool still night/The stars shown bright/Some sight". I have to say that the beauty found in this spot is never disappointing. There is a mystical flavor there and Dad expresses his awe of it all in this poem. He seems alone in his meditation over his sensual experience of the day, and, especially at the day's end, when he seems to find solace in nature's beauty and serenity, in spite of whether or not he shares his experience with anyone else. It almost seems he was alone all this time, and I wonder if, although Mom was physically present, she wasn't there in spirit with him. It is only after all this that he does share with his reader, whoever that may be.

Thanks For [1-25-87]

Thanks

For

Being you plus all you do.

Being kind your natural state of mind.

Being forebearing [forbearing] & understanding.

Being there for every family care.

Seeing to each daily need

and every feed.

In tender silence you fill my every

need.

Kerk [with] love   *I don't want to talk about it.*
1-25-87   *Senior citizens need lots of love too.*

It seems Dad wrote this poem while at The Registry Hotel on the room's stationary. Again, it is difficult to determine whether he is alone or not. He surrounds the hotel logo with two postscripts–"I don't want to talk about/it." [and] "Senior citizens need lots of love too". However, the main body of the poem seems an attempt to instill a sense of well-being in Mom. Each line lists a positive attribute. The first four lines begin with the word "Being" and the fifth with the word "Seeing". Dad showers her with compliments of all sorts-for all that she does, for her kindness-which he describes as her "natural state of mind", her forbearance and understanding, and all she does for her family. Forbear is (#106, pg. 564, 1. to refrain from; avoid doing or saying. 2.to keep oneself in check; to control oneself) and this was surely accurate regarding Mom's disposition. Finally, in the last two lines in the main body of the poem-"In tender silence you fill my every/need". He signs off Kerk [with love] 1-25-87

    I wonder about her "tender silence" for her silence, I believe, often masked her resentment and in the end, led to her emotional demise. The two lines surrounding the hotel logo are also telling-"I don't want to talk about/it" and underneath, "Senior citizens need lots of love too". Were Dad's amorous intentions rebuked that night at the Registry Hotel or beforehand? Does he count himself among the class of senior citizens "who need lots of love too"? If she was with him on this trip it seems nothing of this sort occurred on this particular night, does it?

Wish [9-19-87]
You felt better
more of the time.
Might that you would
become more sublime.
Scars of the past
Oh dissapear [disappear]
Sadness of the past
is best left behind.
Consentrate [concentrate] only on
the best of Times.

> *Since you poses [possess] more*
> *Beauty of body and mind*
> *Than almost [all] other*
> *live womenkind [womankind].*
> Kerk. 9-19-87

The title "Wish" is actually the first word in this poem.-"Wish you felt better/more of the time". Next, Dad continues- "Might that you would/become more sublime". This is his wish for her. He elaborates on her torment and possible remedy for her to find the sublime-"Scars of the past/Oh disappear/Sadness of the past is best left behind". Dad refers here to Mom's difficult childhood. I do believe that this compromised her relationships with all her family members. It dampened her ability to connect with others on an emotional level. I don't believe she really found peace until she lost her mind in the end. At least, I hope she found peace.

In lines nine and ten, when Dad gives his advise, his tendency to misspell words is becoming more apparent. Examples are his spelling of concentrate, possess and womankind. By this time, he might have already been compromised by the dementia that eventually killed him. However, he maintained his insight until the very end of his life, in spite of the fact that he lost almost all ability to speak. It was his sophisticated use of facial expressions that allowed him to communicate effectively-again until the very end.

The last part of this poem has a focus on advice and flattery. His advise was for her to "Concentrate only on/the best of times" and his flattery followed-"Since you possess more/beauty of body and mind/than almost [any] other of womankind".

Jean- [K-9-21-87]

I love you
Your form
Your grace
Your ever
Lovely face.
The extacy [ecstasy] of
Your embrace
Indellably [Indelibly]
In place
My total being
To embrace
K-9-21-87
Always thinking of you
2:00 A.M. Reno
Tears
In my ears

This poem was written only a few days after the last, and is very similar in content to "Wish". He emits an element of personal melancholy over his wife's plight. He continues to make attempts to bolster her self-esteem. We see here the same type of flattery and encouragement.

It seems Dad is in Reno this time, on his own. It is 2:00 A.M. and he is awake-dreaming of his wife. His poem showers her with compliments that cover her physical and soulful beauty-"I love you/Your form/Your grace/Your ever/Lovely face". Next, he pivots to their physical and emotional bond-He reminisces about "the ecstasy of/ [her] embrace" which is fused "indelibly/In place" in his mind. And finally, he writes to her that his "total being" embraces the indelible memory of her essence.

Along the right margin of this poem, Dad pens a postscript-"Always thinking of you". It is "2:00 A.M. [in] Reno" and he is alone with his thoughts and fantasy. His melancholy associated with all this is evident, for he adds another sentiment-"Tears/In my ears". His tears are un-tethered and they run into his ears.

An Answer [4-25-88]
How beautiful life is from
the outside looking in.
Simplicities uncomplicated
Niceties in panoramic view.
Quiet times of harmony espied.
Aspen leaf in a breeze
Peace of mind
From the outside looking in
Is easy to find momentarily
But to hold for a prolonged
period [,] that [']s the question
And the answer is death.
Kerk.
4-25-88

Dad starts out with the two lines-"How beautiful life is from/ the outside looking in." He sets the stage for the reader to wonder where he is going with this. He doesn't say life is beautiful from the inside looking out, which would suggest that the beauty in life is found from within-the typical manner in which one's brain makes sense of the world at large. Instead, it's the other way around. What is external stimulation ("the outside" or the separate from the individual) is what matters most. He sees life's beauty in nature, which influences his appreciation of it. In his mind, at least in this poem, it seems that the human experience is dependent on what's outside of us, not the other way around. But by taking it all in, it becomes a part of us-"Simplicities uncomplicated/Niceties in panoramic view./Quiet times of harmony espied". Espy is (#107, pg. 496, to catch sight of; make out; spy; descry). For instance, his meditative sight of the "Aspen leaf in a breeze/[provides] Peace of mind." He elaborates on this thought-"From the outside looking in/is easy to find [peace] momentarily/But to hold for a prolonged/period [,] that ['] s the question/And the answer is death."

I believe he anticipates a shift at death, for although there are glimpses of the sublime in life while "looking from the outside in", at death life's limitations are left behind. Life on earth has its difficulties that get in the way. However, what was momentary in life becomes "prolonged" in death, for the soul is set free-untethered by the temporal state of being-and there is the unification of awareness-outside and inside become one. What was a momentary peace of mind for him will become everlasting peace.

Mind Set to Rose [5-1-88]
Mind program set in youth
Unconsciously incendentally [incidentally].
Fused inperceptably [imperceptibly].
Non consequential Trivia
magnified.
Color the future improperly
into a gray black hue

Analyze
the words match them to the
offending deeds.
See
The folly of the guilt.
Re-hue color anew
Imbued a new Tint [-] the Rose is you.
Kerk. 5-1-88

During this period of time in Mom and Dad's lives the topic of Mom's emotional state comes up repeatedly in Dad's poetry. He writes over and over to boost her self esteem and pronounce his love. In spite of his attempts, nothing ever seemed to penetrate the wall of guilt and insecurity that permeated Mom's being. In this poem, he starts out- "Mind program set in youth/Unconsciously incidentally/Fused imperceptibly." He is writing of messages Mom told of receiving in her childhood and youth, predominantly from her own mother. We kids got wind of some of this, but, for the most part, Dad was the recipient of her woes. I believe he had become more and more aware of the damage he felt was done to Mom. He was her champion in this regard. In this poem, he lays out his understanding of her emotional demise and makes an attempt to sway her: "Mind program set in youth"-she was brain washed, in his estimation. She is unaware of the subtlety of her mother's warfare-"Unconsciously incidentally" and the result- the damage was "fused [to her] imperceptibly [by her]". Incidentally is (#108, pg. 736, 1. in an incidental manner; by chance; accidentally) so her mother's behavior towards her had incidental repercussions. He goes on to describe ways in which she was undermined-"Non-consequential Trivia" was used to wear her down and then "magnified". The result is that she has "Color[ed] the future improperly/into a gray black hue". She sees the world and herself through this lens.

The rest of this poem is his attempt to repair, in some manner, the damage done long ago. He suggests she "Analyze" what occurred. He asks her to recognize "the words" spoken to her and "match them to the/offending deeds". If she recognizes the discrepancy, she will "See/The folly of the guilt" she holds so dear. He adds one other suggestion, that she "Re-hue [a] color anew/Imbued a new Tint the Rose is you". Imbue is (#109, pg. 725, 2. to fill with color. 3. to fill (the mind, etc.); permeate; pervade; inspire (with principles, feelings, emotions, etc.). This is what he hopes for her, that she will "see' the world through a different lens-instead of "a gray black hue" she will recognize herself in relation to a "color anew", and when she is "imbued" with this new vibrant color, she will see herself as the beautiful Rose that he sees.

Soft You Are [5-13-88]
Soft You Are
Soft of heart [,] of touch
Love you so much
tender in your mind
With a heart so so fine
And-You ['] r [e] partly mine
Oh life can be so de vine [divine]
The verse is short
and small
My love for you to me is all

See you
In N.Y. tonight
God willing

that I can give
So long as I will live.
Friday
Kerk 5-13-88
Can you read my Script.
tonight

Here again, there is not much time between this poem's creation and the last. Dad must be waiting for Mom to arrive and join him in NYC. At the left-hand top of the page he writes a brief note above this poem–"See you/in N.Y. tonight/God willing". He often qualified a statement of his with a potential rebuttal of his expected outcome for he always considered the realistic notion that one never knows what might occur when one expects a certain outcome. As he got older, this trait of his became more and more commonplace. Every time we would have a family get-together, upon someone's departure, he would announce that "this just might be the last time we ever see each other". Anyway, in this case, he prepared himself for the potential that something or anything might prevent their reunion.

While Dad waits for their reunion, he daydreams about her. As was also common, he seems enthralled with her softness, both in her demeanor, her temperament and her physically soft body, as compared to his. Dad seems almost giddy with anticipation. In the sixth line of the poem–"And-You're partly mine" he knows that part of her is lost to him, because of her personal torment and secretive nature. But he seems willing to accept this fact and then focuses on what he cherishes about their union–"Oh life can be so de vine [divine]". I suspect he creates a double entendre in this line- "divine" in the conventional sense, but then also what is the best of life-what comes from the fruit of "the vine"- a tribute to their romance that often included a really good bottle of wine that they would share. Unfortunately, as time went by, this became a problem.

In the following two lines he tells her-"The verse is short/and small" but contrasts this statement with how grand his feelings are for her-My love for you to me is all/that I can give/so long as I will live". Next to his signing off, he writes-"Friday/Kerk 5-13-88" and underneath-"Can you read my Script/tonight". He doesn't add a question mark for he anticipates her arrival when she will be able to read the poem and answer him herself.

Erased [no date]
Ran the Ocean-wasn't any message left in the snow
Sand-prints all wiped clean
Realized then all
Erased like evanescent dreams
Imperfect solitude [,] your spell descends
While alone without a friend
Stare
Empty space
Surf pounding at every visible place
Solitude erased
Melancholy replaced
by steady beats as each perfect wave thrusts
then repeats
Slowly the sand shift to end the empty blend
Bliss reimbraced [re-embraced]

Satisfied reality returned

Embraced daydreams replaced with age ['] s aches and

Pains even in this blissful place

then

perfect pounding symphony dispells [dispels] all-and ends.

I grow tearful reading over this poem. There is a sense of his loneliness throughout. He tells of his run along the beach, describing scenes, emotions and ideas that erupt. First, he notices the snow-covered beach where no written messages or footprints survived- "Sand-prints all wiped clean". He continues in this vein-"Realized then all/Erased like evanescent dreams". Evanescent is (#110, pg. 502, tending to fade from sight; vanishing; ephemeral). This is just the way our dreams vanish or escape us upon wakening. The magnitude of the ocean tides render the sand-prints insignificant, just as our dreams disappear as if they weren't ever there.

In the fifth line, he finds that his observations lead to "Imperfect solitude". Its "spell descends/While alone without a friend". A spell is (#111, pg. 1401, 2. magical power or irresistible influence; charm; fascination) and its synonym magic is (#112, pg. 881, 2. any mysterious, seemingly inexplicable, or extraordinary power or influence). This spell-a natural or supernatural force-takes hold of him, and perhaps annihilates him, at least temporarily. The next two lines describe the result-"Stare/Empty space"-obliteration. But then, in the next line, there is a change. He again becomes aware of the "Surf pounding at every visible place" and his "solitude [is] erased". His "Melancholy [is] replaced/by steady beats as each perfect wave thrusts/then repeats/Slowly the sand shift to end the empty blend/[and] Bliss [is] re-embraced". He is one with nature.

Bliss is (#113, pg. 157, 2. spiritual joy; heavenly rapture) and so "satisfied reality [is] returned". He becomes engaged in the power of nature surrounding him again and is again able to connect to his surroundings and the wonder of it all.

But, yet again, in the last four lines, there is a juxtaposition of his two themes-annihilation and eternity. His "embraced daydreams [are] replaced with age ['] s aches and/Pains even in this blissful place/[and] then/[a] perfect pounding symphony dispels all-and ends. Dispel is (#114, pg. 421, to scatter and drive away; cause to vanish; disperse). The tide's force continues to change the landscape and finally the waves make what is present vanish. It all ends. He recognizes his mortality with his "aches and pains", even in the presence of "this blissful place." He even questions the sea, with its "perfect pounding symphony" that might continue on forever. However, in his last line, even the "perfect pounding symphony"- the rhythm of the sea's waves may have its own demise-it dispels all-and ends. And then what happens? Does the ocean, with its seeming uninterrupted movement, have the same fate as he will have?

Postscript: In this poem Dad is at the beach with conditions he has described in past poems, when the beach is snow covered. It is the winter of his life. He questions whether anything will remain of him, similar to the ever changing forces of nature. I really believe that his poetry writing was an attempt to leave some sort of mark, even though, in the end, all memory of his existence will be obliterated anyway. The flavor of this poem is unlike some of his others which propose a more optimistic and spiritual rendition of reality.

With Jean [Dec. 11]
Quiet time of life we are in
Less fuss than in our youth has been
Peaceful naps for me easily begin
After a casual luncheon
Off to bed- nestle down
To restlessly toss around
Till bird songs at dawn
Call us from bed to bound
Still wonderful to see you around
With the love we have found
Let it last as it has in the past.
Dec. 11
F.R.K.

Although there is no year to this poem's date, I believe it was written in 1988 due to the placement in the album. This was not long before Dad retired at age sixty-two because I suspect he was feeling his age in all sorts of ways. He starts out-"Quiet time of life we are in"-this quite the contrast to their lives earlier on. Dad was so full of vigor for most of his life up to this point and Mom made a valiant effort to keep up with him. But now, things are different. He reflects on the changes and seems to accept his aging, but maybe not really enthusiastic about it. He notes the changes to their lives in the poem-"Less fuss than in our youth has been/ Peaceful naps for me easily begin/After a casual luncheon". I have to say that Dad never had any trouble dropping off throughout the day from as early on as I can remember. It was the nights that kept him up, a perpetual insomniac, and he makes mention of this in the next few lines-"Off to bed-nestle down/To restlessly toss around/Till bird songs at dawn/Call us from bed to bound". "To bound" could mean leaping out of bed, or another interpretation, to be under compulsion to rise. Mom wasn't a great sleeper either and here he may be suggesting that neither of them is eager to wake up and start the day.

In the last three lines, he changes focus to their relationship-"Still wonderful to see you around/With the love we have found". This declaration doesn't seem to me as enthusiastic as it might have in the past. The passion seems to have slipped away a bit and what may have taken its place is complacent familiarity and companionship. He ends with-"Let it last as it has in the past". There seems to be a note of misgiving or doubt about their future.

Jean The [1-8-89]

[Jean The] Rose in the family without a thorn

Why starrey [starry] eyes were you born

It's on the wall for everyone to see

The four belonging to you and me

Chiseled set the entire clan

Satisfaction predestined since it began

Having earned happiness and peace

Hope the future grants you these.

Were I God I would heed all you pleas.

Those you request while on your knees.

by-Bobby

1-8-89

For Jeanie

Love Poems and Obsession

Here we have a new year and a title similar to the last poem's title. Really, this title continues with the first word of the first line-"Rose", hence, "Jean The Rose". This isn't the first time he has likened her to a rose. It has been a theme throughout the collection. In this one, he tells her that she is a "Rose in the family without a thorn". I think here he separates her from the rest of our nuclear family, for he saw her without the character flaws he sees in himself and his progeny. Next, he asks-"Why starry eyes were you born"-He was always smitten with the beauty of her eyes but I also think here he alludes to the faraway look in them too. She often seemed in her own world, hence, "starry eyes".

The next four lines focus on their progeny. He adds the line- "Why starry eyes were you born"-what do they give away and what happened to create them? Then-"It's on the wall for everyone to see/The four belonging to you and me/Chiseled set the entire clan/Satisfaction predestined since it began". I think here he is referring to the photographs on the wall that portray a certain "Chiseled" appearance of familial similarity. Chiseled is (#115, pg. 256, 2. finely wrought, as if shaped by a chisel; well-formed). But that's not all, for he hints that the starry appearance is also evident in all. Somehow, their progeny inherited the same kind of eyes. In the next line, he tells her and the reader that "Satisfaction [was] predestined" for their union. In his mind, they couldn't have produced anything but magnificence. I didn't say it, he did- but I guess it's nice that he felt that way.

In the last four lines he returns to a focus on her. He tells her that the rest of the family has "earned happiness and peace" and he hopes the same for her-"Hope the future grants you these [things]".

Then he tells her he hopes she finds the same, and if he was God he "would heed her pleas/those you request while [praying] on your knees". This was something she did a lot. He knew that his prayers hadn't been answered, but if he could have changed things for her, he would have.

He signs off "by-Bobby" and calls her "Jeanie"-both names are terms of endearment for each other and reminiscent of their youth.

Ocean Scene [5-89]
View was Supreme
As you Jean lovely thing
Were [Where?] you could not have been
[Had] Duty not supreme [Because duty is supreme]
Beranger Beaujolais 87
Fifth-with food was heaven
Bowl of tiny steamer clams
Good almost as your
Succulent being
But the best on the menu
For you was not of venue
Since for you poached salmon
Is not but a lemon
Think of you when you ['] re not here
Don't die Before me dear K-
5-89

I think, in this poem, Dad daydreams again about Mom after a meal he has alone. He writes to her that the "View was Supreme/ As you Jean [,] lovely thing"- his view of her is as lovely as the ocean scene. Then tells her-"Were [Where] you could not have been/ [had Duty not [been] supreme". I suspect what he tries to say here, as I suggest above, is that she could not be there with him because of her allegiance to her kin, which is a priority for her in his mind. We don't know what it was that left her behind. Next, he describes his meal in detail, maybe as a way of sharing it with her, even in her absence. He describes the choice of wine-"Beranger Beaujolais '87" and that the food that accompanied it was "heaven", such as "[the] bowl of tiny steamer clams" that he proclaims are almost as good as her "succulent being"-an obvious sexual implication. Next he writes that "But the best on the menu/ For you was not of venue/Since for you poached salmon/is not but a lemon". Mom wasn't fond of salmon, and he knows that a salmon dish for her offers little more than the slice of lemon. I'm unsure about his use of the word venue? One definition is (#116, pg. 478, (WPD) the place or setting of an action or event). So, in this context, he may be implying that this particular restaurant, which featured a salmon dish, was not the right place for her to have been that evening, but he obviously enjoyed it. Finally, he expresses his feeling of loneliness there at the beach without her-"Think of you when you're not here", so much so that he recognizes that if she was gone for good, he would be in deep emotional trouble. This leads to the final line-"Don't die before me dear"-for he feels he couldn't live without her, and he didn't have to.

I See Not-So Hot [6-7-89]
Sorry when
I fortuitously make you sad
Happy when
Such makes you glad.

Cheryl Krkoč

When you ail
My
Psyche goes pale.
Unable To help
I dispair [despair].
Your spirit
in disarrey [disarray]
Forty down
about twenty to go.   *Need your glasses*
Let ['] s try   *for this one.*
to make the best
Of the
rest of the show
Might I
change myself.
Open
the door
And let
your heart talk more
Of the
complex being
Hard for
my seeing.
Things far
Ago in the past
Great
differences cast
But one

Love Poems and Obsession

fact endures
Body and soul
I really am yours.
6-7-89

R.E. Morris pen name
for F.R.K. today

It seems this title tells us that Dad doesn't see (understand) his mate so well-"I See Not So Hot". The body of the poem explores this further. He apologizes for his shortcoming-"Sorry when/I fortuitously make you sad". Fortuitous is (#117, pg. 570, happening by chance; accidental). But then, he is "Happy when/ such makes you glad. I guess the "such" is used for whatever it is that makes her glad. I suppose he might come upon just the right way to please her, but then, he could also please her merely by happenstance. It seems here he admits that he often doesn't know what he's doing when faced with understanding or pleasing the opposite sex. Another factor he has to cope with is her fragile psyche and his bewilderment about how to reach her-"When you ail /My psyche goes pale/Unable to help/I despair/ [because] your spirit/ [is] in disarray". Next, he reminds her that there are "Forty down/about twenty to go". He speaks here of their forty years union. They married on September 3rd of 1949 and this poem was written in 1989. He predicts they'll have maybe twenty more. In fact, they had twenty-three, but not all of it went well. Dad always was good at predictions. He did well in the stock market because he was good at paying attention to trends. He had insight about a lot of other things too, but predicting Mom was another matter altogether.

Next, he makes a suggestion-"Let ['] s try/to make the best/ of the/rest of the show". It is as if he sees their lives together as something he might see on stage or in a movie. It's a story he tells here, a personal history that is playing out in real time. He asks himself a question next-"Might I change myself/Open the door/And let your heart talk more/of the complex being/hard for my seeing [?]" He was the big talker in their relationship, and sometimes, I believe, his talkativeness thwarted her voice. He seems to have finally recognized this about himself and her. He also calls her a "complex being" that is "hard for [his] seeing". Even if he makes a concerted effort to listen to her more carefully, he wonders if this will allow her to open up to him and that he will understand. He analyzes the situation-"Things [about her life] far ago in the past/Great differences [between their personalities] cast"-are potential barriers. Finally, he wants to reassure her-"But one fact endures/Body and soul I really am yours." He did learn to listen, to reach out to her, and I do believe she opened up to him. In spite of this, though, she seemed to have had a difficult time letting go of her past.

Dad writes a little note on the right hand margin-"Need your glasses for/This one". I guess he thought his cursive was smaller than usual. At the bottom right hand margin he signs off-"R.E. Morris pen name/for F.R.K. today/6-7-89. He tells of the type of fountain pen he wrote this poem with. He liked fountain pens the best and they encouraged a flourish to his writing as well as a tendency for the print to be smaller than usual. He signs off with his initials-F.R.K. for Frank Roberto Krkoč, and the date-6-7-89.

Frances a Lass [2-16-90]
Without an "I" in her name.
We who know you understand same.

Face angelically Framing deep lovely eyes
Racing mind tending others with more than sighs
Around always aiding all family members in need.
Never shirking duties to products of her seed.
Caring year after year happily chronically Tired.
Endlessly spending life mind love inspired
Sleep in peace to end only in heaven retired.
With love K 2-16-90

Frances is Mom's first given name-after her father Franz-but she usually went by her middle name-Jean. In this instance, Dad decides to use her first name in the title of the poem and as a compass for its content-note that her name is spelled out in the left margin of lines three through nine, and he underlines the first letter in each of these lines to emphasize what he has done. It also looks as though he used a ruler to make each line straight and with some semblance of a heart shape to this poem. The first line tells the reader that her name is the feminine version of the masculine counterpart-Francis-one version of the masculine form of the name. Others are Frank, Dad's name, and Franz, the German form of the name that was her father's. I think, here, he is differentiating her from the male versions as an indication that her role in life is different from the males close to her. He starts out writing-"We who know you understand same"-that is, they know that she is the very different feminine version of her male counterparts. She is unquestionably feminine.

Dad goes on to classify and elaborate on these gender differences. First, he tells of her feminine appearance that he seems smitten with-"Face angelically Framing deep lovely eyes"-he sees her physicality as some form of an angel. Next, he moves on to other feminine attributes. In his mind, she has a "racing mind" because of all the feminine duties she has to perform that make her harried. She is "…tending to others with more than sighs"-he believes-that although it is difficult for her, she tends to her family gladly-"with more than sighs" but may also suggest that she carries on her duties somewhere between enthusiasm and resignation. She is also "Around always aiding all family members in need" and "Never shirking duties to products of her seed"-we kids. All this "Caring year after year" is done "happily" and leads to her being "chronically tired" and "endlessly spending [her] life mind [and] love inspired". He sees this calling as an inspiration for her, but really though, happily? Inspiration is (#118, pg. 757, 3. an inspiring influence; any stimulus to creative thought or action).

Dad may have written this poem about the time that Mom asked us kids to ignore Mother's Day. It seemed she had the idea that she wasn't a very good mother, and her own feelings about her mother seemed also to play a part in her request. Maybe Dad was trying to bolster her confidence by writing this poem about her devotion to her family. I do think Mom was aware of her shortcomings as a parent and Dad seems to have unintentionally pointed this out in this poem. He describes here a woman carrying out her duties but maybe without the enthusiasm one might expect. In his telling, it sounds very much like a life of drudgery. It also seems, as he describes her, that her driving force in caring for her family is duty, which he names in line six. In line seven he describes her as "chronically tired" and in line four "tending to others with more than sighs". There is no end in sight for her in this poem, for she will "sleep in peace to end only in heaven retired". There will be no end of her responsibility until her death. It will be only then that she will rest.

I think that Mom's generation was a transitional one. Before WWII, in The United States, women were generally home raising a family. Women who didn't marry were usually delegated to the professions of nurse or elementary school teacher-really an extension of the typical female role in society. Mom seemed, to me, often lost in the shuffle of our family dynamic. Dad was charismatic, extroverted, at least in his early years, and, of course, a male in this era of male dominance. She had ambition to attend college but that was denied her because of her mother's assumed feeling that this would have been a threat to her. So she sabotaged Mom's aspirations. Mom was a kind mother, but I don't think she was a happy mother. I don't think she found the role to be fulfilling. I think if she had been born into another era, things may have been quite different for her, any children she might have had, and even different and possibly better for her husband.

Life Sentence [07-7 & 8-90]
Who is to blame? Let ['] s play a game.
At one messy pants
Naughty girl
At two a single error
Bad thing
At three her they did not see
At four who permanently close the door
At five one Time she childlessy [childishly] lied
At six no use again just never tried

At seven as always she would blindly mind
At eight her loyalty did not really matter.
By nine [she was] constantly sadder.
By ten [,] confusion was the norm.
By eleven she guessed she did not belong.
By twelve her heart held only a sad song
By thirteen guilt permanently set
By fourteen very little heart left
By fifteen body and spirit Bent.
Seeping slowly with the years
The last of hope drops with the tears.
Wonder if there is one to caress
Does it end as such for this sweet lass.
To [too?] long for permanent release
From a verdict wrongly pressed
Upon a guiltless one that was so o-pressed
How sad is there no reprieve
From such irrationality but death
Or clense [cleanse] yourself with my tears please
Kerk
07-7 & 8-90

In the left margin of this poem Dad writes "[poem] Comes with hanky & Rose.", and "[cutout of an Apple]of my eye" and "past midnight"-when this poem was written.

In right margin he writes "Sweet dreams- [for my] Sweet dream." and "Need your glasses for this one."-again, referring to his small print.

This poem is a soliloquy and seems to have a similar subject matter as the previous poem, "Frances a Lass". The title, "Life Sentence", suggests there was judgment and punishment of some sort cast upon the main character in this poem-Mom. Dad describes what he has uncovered about Mom's past based on conversations the two had about this topic. The previous poem casts her in the light of a self sacrificing caregiver, and hints at her discontent in this role. I believe Dad tries to connect her life sentence of domestic servitude in "Frances a Lass" to her upbringing, at least in part. And now he presents evidence of the connection between her current role and her childhood and adolescence.

He starts out with the question-"Who is to blame?" and "Let's play a game". Every year from age one to fifteen is examined, in the first half of this poem, by a one or two line phrase that describes a shaming event-"at one messy pants/Naughty girl", At Two a single error/Bad thing", At three her they did not see", at four who permanently closed the door". He estimates here that this is when something in her was broken and she shut down-"closed the door". "At five one Time she childishly lied" (and got a spanking for it). "At six no use again just never tried"-she gives up her self against the odds. By the age of seven she would "…as always …blindly mind"-no fight left. At eight her loyalty did not really matter"-there was nothing to get her on her mother's good side. "By nine constantly sadder"-her emotional condition deteriorates. "By ten confusion was the norm"-What am I supposed to do or say?" "By eleven she guessed she did not belong"-she found no champions in her household". "By twelve her heart held only a sad song"-her integrity is thwarted. "By thirteen guilt permanently set/By fourteen very little heart left"-She claims a life-long guilt and her heart is broken. Then-"By fifteen body and spirit Bent"-and finally, hope "Seeping [away] slowly with the years/The last of hope drops with the tears". With his use of the word "bent", I think he implies that she cannot stand up straight under the pressure of all that criticism and abuse. Bent also can mean (#119, pg. 138, adj. 3. set in a course. n. 1. an inclination; tendency). Both definitions seem to apply. Finally, with her spirit bent, "the last of hope drops with her tears". Her lost hope and tears are intertwined, for as her tears drop, so does her hope and her loss of hope brings on the tears.

The remainder of the poem changes course. Dad looks for some solution. He looks for what might be his role in helping her heal. He asks himself the question-"Wonder if there is one to caress". Might he be her salvation if he is able to get through to her? But he seems to have doubts because he has already tried to cajole her with kind words and encouragement. Next, he asks himself, "Does it end as such for this sweet lass. Lass is (#120, pg. 824, origin and derivation from Anglo-N., "not bound". 1. a young woman, girl. 2. sweetheart). I suspect Dad continued to see Mom as a young woman or girl, maybe because she never fully developed emotionally. But she remained his "sweetheart" for good. Next-"To long for permanent release/From a verdict wrongly pressed". He seems to be trying to answer the question he asked-"Does it end as such". Is the answer for her "to long for permanent release" and achieve this? Or was the phrase meant as "Too long [a time has passed] for a permanent release/From a verdict wrongly pressed". Is it too late for her to change? Is the ill conceived verdict she received, sustained from her youth, indestructible even though

Love Poems and Obsession

it was "wrongly pressed/Upon a guiltless one that was o-pressed [oppressed]"-being wrongly pressed led to her being oppressed or o-pressed. Next, he comments on his concern that there may be only one way for her to be released from her condition-"How sad is there no reprieve/From such irrationality but death [?]" which he has questioned in previous poems. He may be assigning some responsibility to her for her predicament when he uses the word "irrationality". Was she, in part, participating in propagating her "irrational" belief system or even exhibiting some sort of perverse satisfaction in maintaining her miserable state? Dad offers up an alternative in the final line-"Or cleanse yourself with my tears please"-for his tears might be a form of baptism of sorts-to cleanse her soul, to wash away her guilt and make her new. He will offer up his own suffering for her to heal-maybe much like a Jesus figure.

Post script. The side-lines in each margin compliment the text of this poem. In the left margin he tells her that the poem "Comes [with] hanky & [a] Rose. He anticipates tears may fall with the reading, hence the hanky, and the rose is to show his love and support. The "apple of my eye" seems playful and a declaration of his feelings for her. The last in the right margin wants to let her know that it was past midnight when he penned this poem. On the right margin he writes-"Sweet dreams-Sweet dream". He hopes there will be sweet dreams for his sweet dream-her. The last ditty is "Need your glasses for this one". He has written this in another margin before. This, it seems, when his writing is small.

Demise [10-28-90]
Belly's bloated was blurted out
Tender hand depart

Elated voice drops low
Disappointments flow
Alas no martini glow
Error un-retrievable
In an unbelievable stew
Mistake-love you
Know such moments
are regrettable few
That ['] s one I blew
Love Kerk 10-28-90

In this poem Dad describes killing the mood with a thoughtless comment-"Belly's bloated was blurted out"-not something any woman would want to hear about herself and Dad was often found making not-well-thought-out-comments. The result-"Tender hand depart [s]"-she is hurt and angry. Her once "Elated voice drops low"-another bad sign. Then "Disappointments flow"-not only her disappointment at a ruined pleasant evening together, but his too, and as a result-"Alas no martini glow" that both were anticipating. Dad reckons that the "Error [is] un-retrievable"-it's too late. He finds himself "In an unbelievable stew". Finally, he admonishes himself away from future screw-ups-"Mistake-love you/Know such moments/are regrettable few/That's one I blew"- his apology to her.

My Heart [2-18-91]
Back in forty one
Saw a perky bit of sun
Rose again in forty six
Heart played tricks

Love Poems and Obsession

> *Mind too*
> *Then*
> *Know then what to do*
> *Marry you*
> *Close now is sunset time*
> *Retrospect sublime*
> *For heart and mind*
> *It could be an eternal find*
> *Late Valentine Bob 2-18-91*

In this poem Dad describes the beginnings of his relationship with Mom. The older he got, the more often he waxed poetic (verbally) about their intermittent courtship. Their first encounter was at their high school lockers where he asked to see her report card, which he often proclaimed with glee had all A's. He starts his poem-"Back in forty one/Saw a perky bit of sun". In 1941 Mom was thirteen and he was fifteen. In those days photos of her sometimes caught her with a spirited expression and devil-may-care attitude-hence, Dad's description-"...a perky bit of sun". Then the relationship "Rose again in [19] forty six"-they met again after Dad returned to the U.S. after WWII. He recalled often how he reacted to his chance meeting with her. She was working at the Elmhurst College campus malt chop and he resuming his studies there after his stint in the Navy. Next, he describes this surprise reunion-"Heart played tricks/Mind too/then/Know then what to do/Marry you". It seems he was love-struck. She was mesmerizing to him.

Next, he brings focus back to the present with the following lines-"Close now [compared to then] is sunset time/Retrospect sublime" for he gets to relive their life together so far and it feels "sublime/for heart and mind". Finally, his melding of past and present leads him to the final refrain-""It could be an eternal find". This sentiment of his that their love will live on into eternity is a frequent occurrence in his love poems. He signs off-"Late Valentine" and then "Bob 2-18-91"-four days late. (He writes this poem on Four Seasons Hotel Stationary).

Difference [5-20-91]
Hard to understand
Harder to learn
Each marching to
Ones own band.
Our fires others burn
Escaping the lighters hand
Others ways are hard to
grasp.
Like handfuls of dry
sand.
In time one hopes to be
At least a player in
the others band.
But if love is a partner
In the batter
Does it really matter?
No!
Sequence
Minor consequence
No real difference.

Love Bobby K
5-20-91

In this poem Dad speculates about the differences between people, and, in particular, between himself and his wife. He starts out-"Hard to understand/ [and even] harder to learn/ [because] each [of us are] marching to/Ones own band". In the next two lines-"Our fires [cause] others [to] burn/Escaping the lighters hand"-so the one who lights the fire with the lighter is spared the burn to his hand, telling the reader that one individual's passion or "fires" can "burn others", for only he or she has control of his or her own intentions. I think he speaks here of his fiery temperament-not always easy to bear and maybe also her quiet reserve and anger. He turns then to a more literal explanation-"Others ways are hard to/grasp./Like handfuls of dry/sand." I like this metaphor-for "handfuls of dry sand" are surely hard to hold on to, in fact, impossible. Will they ever really grasp the other's essence? Then-"In time one hopes to be/At least a player in/the others band." He has returned to the theme of the first four lines. This opens a chance for a greater degree of understanding. In the next line, he changes course again. His question to himself is-"But if love is a partner/In the batter/Does it really matter?" Batter is (#121, pg. 125, 1. to beat or strike with blow after blow). The word also sounds like "battle" and both connote a kind of contest or injury-the challenge of living itself. He answers the question "Does it really matter?" with a resounding "No!" for "...if love is a partner/In the batter [or battle]" then love will overcome any misunderstanding or harm done. Finally, he comes to the conclusion-"Sequence/Minor consequence/No real difference". So any sequence of events will have a result that follows-the consequence, maybe a minor misunderstanding, but in the end love will prevail-at least, he hopes so.

You. [7-12-94]
You know I will think of
you,
Many times each day of
you.
Walking, running, walking
of you
And with coctails [cocktails] too
of you-
then a tear or two
appear for you.
(over)
Bobby Love You Always
7-12-94

This little note was written on a gift care titled "Happy Birthday", signed 7-12-94-six days before Mom's real birthday on July 18th. The poem's title is "You" for that is the topic of this poem-no surprise here. "You know I will think of/you/Many times each day of you." Very romantic, I think. He is doing this daydreaming about her while "Walking, running, walking" and while having "cocktails too". These lines all end with "[thinking] of you" until the final two lines that change the tone somewhat, but also alters the fabric of the entire poem-"then a tear or two/appear for you". There is this hint of sadness about their separation attached to his adoration of her. He decorates the card with penning of little hearts with small circles beneath them. They look like circles that often accompany a thought of a character in the funny pages, only instead of a bubble, a heart holds the sentiment. He signs off "Bobby" and adds "Love You Always" on the back of the card that I assume accompanied a gift of flowers.

To Thee [7-18-91]
Beautiful Wife
Delight of my life
Shy Butterfly
Glint in my eye
Happy hello
Heart a-glow
Of love –I know
Gift from above
Short simple poem
To one I love
Happy 63rd 7-18-91 Bobby

This poem was written on Mom's exact birthday, unlike the last. It seems to be written on hotel stationary. It's hard to tell if he was away or at home, as he often scavenged hotel sundries for home use. The title "To Thee" leads to the text-"Beautiful Wife/Delight of my life/Shy Butterfly/"-She was that, and so different than he. Next he writes that she is a "glint in my eye"-Glint is synonymous with a gleam and/or a glimpse. Gleam is (#122, n., pg. 615, 1. a momentary brightness; flash or beam of light; 2. to appear or be revealed suddenly). He speaks of the shine in her eyes that reflect into his. I also think he alludes to this glint in his eye being the result of tearfulness which can appear as brightness; the teary eye reflecting his adoration. In the fifth line there is a shift- "Happy hello" which introduces his anticipation of or delight in their reunion, and then emphasized by the next two lines-"Heart A-glow/Of love-I know". She is a "Gift from above". He signs off-"Short simple poem/To [the] one I love" and finally-"Happy 63rd 7-18-91 Bobby"

Yourself [8-20-91]

To Jean with Tears

Your eyes don't see
Your ears don't hear
But inside
Inner feelings of fear
that are not clear
Perceptions erroneously
Imprinted
Personality
In youth traumatically
Ah! Outside eyes see
Outside ears hear
And with gut reality
embrace
the true inner grace
Yourself
Bobby
8-20-91

On either side of the title of this poem Dad writes "To Jean" in the left margin and "with Tears" in the right. He lets the reader know right off that this poem reflects his distress. The topic, again, is of Mom's own muddle. He writes- "Your eyes don't see/Your ears don't hear [the truth of the matter]". "But inside/Inner feelings of fear/that are not clear"-to either of them, but especially not to her. We have seen this topic in his poetry many times over. Next, he speculates about the cause of her muddle-" [Her] Perceptions/erroneously/Imprinted" and her "Personality/In youth traumatically" [...]-the thought is interrupted with an "Ah!"-an exclamation of insight-and then goes on to describe his newfound perception of her-"[his]Outside [of her] eyes see/[his]Outside [of her] ears hear" and he even claims a "gut reality" that contributes to his insight. He sees her for what she is minus her own perception of herself. He sees her and hears her. He feels her with his "gut reality"-the truth of her being-and asks her to embrace "the true inner grace/ [Her] self"-this true inner grace that she must come to recognize. He hopes to be her savior. He signs off-"Bobby".

To Me [5-(10-11) 94]
Super fine lady so demure
Damsel sweet and pure
Giving more
Taking less
Embodyment [Embodiment] of unselfishness
Of mind and body in beauty
Born.
With pain and undeserved
Torment born.
May the future yet portend
A fate of better end
Deny all faltless [faultless] guilt
Becoming restless free
To see yourself as
You appear
To me. Bobby 5- (10-11) 94

There is a significant period of time between the writing of this poem and the last-almost three years. Dad seems to write these sentiments just where he left off in the last. The tone and subject matter are so similar. He must have spent two different consecutive days with this one. He asks her, as in the poem "Yourself", to see herself as he sees her-hence, the "to me" is "you are to me" these things I mention. It seems nothing much has changed in Mom's emotional state, but he is resolute in his quest to help her out of her funk. Again, he mentions her tormented childhood, that she seems, in his estimation, unable to discard and almost to a fault. He certainly puts her up on a pedestal except for his hinting at a stubborn-ness on her part to hold on to the past. There is also a tone of exacerbation on his part at his inability to make a difference.

In this poem Dad heaps on compliments as he has done before- "Super fine lady so demure/Damsel sweet and pure/Giving more/Taking less/Embodiment of unselfishness/Of mind and body in beauty/Born". Dad certainly portrays the picture of the ideal female of his time. She is selfness, sacrificing her own desires to concentrate on others. However, Dad seems to miss the price she paid for following the role of the ideal woman. What was missing, as I see it, is that there was never joy in her carrying out the duties of wife and mother in a conventional role. When she was happiest, was when she and he got away for some adventure and she would have his undivided attention. But maybe even this failed her in the long run. I can't know exactly what occurred in her growing up years that scarred her either. I had hints from her but I also know she had secrets she shared with no one at all. So maybe there was nothing Dad could have done to make things better for her. He did try though.

Dad next contrasts the last two lines mentioned with the next two"-With pain and undeserved/Torment born." So she was born in beauty but also born to torment. The rest of the poem is dedicated to his pleas for her to find a way to peace-"May the future yet portend/a fate of better end". Portend is (#123, pg. 1138, to be an omen or warning of; foreshadow; presage) and presage can mean (#124, pg. 1152, 3. to predict). So maybe both apply. He sees the possibility that her current state is a foreshadowing of her future, but he hopes that the future will portend (or predict) "A fate of better end". Finally, he makes a suggestion for her to "Deny all faultless guilt/[and become] restless free/ [and]To see yourself as/you appear/ To me".

Near You [10-28-94]
Want to be near you
My mind near you
Body too near you
Feel the memories of you
Mind pictures appear
when we are apart
Feel content when we
eat, sit, sleep, and
Travel with leasure [leisure]
Meals and Tours
Wine coctails [cocktails] even
Beer are better with you
Hope there is an after

world for us too.
All this and more
Near you
Kerk- 10-28-94

This poem describes Dad's almost addictive-like preoccupation with his amore`. I find it very romantic. Even the title suggests his delight whenever she is in his presence-"Want to be near you/ My mind near you/Body too near you"-mind, body and soul. As he daydreams, he "Feel[s] the memories"-they are as real as when time with her was happening. He elaborates-"Mind pictures appear/when we are apart"-again, not only a memory, but more because it is visceral. He elaborates-"Mind pictures appear/when we are apart/Feel content when we eat, sit, and/Travel with leisure/ Meals and Tours/Wine cocktails even/Beer are better with you". Finally, he looks to the future-"Hope there is an after/world for us too/All this and more/Near you". He doesn't want it to ever end and maybe it didn't.

Signs of Love [12-9-94]
Feel and see them every day.
Things that you don't say
Reflected on as I go on my way
Towels clothes for us to wear
at work or play.
Coffee breakfast lunches smacks
and more
Thought Touches seen everywhere
Floors swept carpet care dishes
to prepare.

> *Apples salads the best to eat*
> *Tenderly chosen one at a time*
> *with all of us in mind.*
> *Done if sick or well*
> *Self sacrifice and prayers for us*
> *Smiles and hugs so fine*
> *Done with eyes that shine*
> *Graceful beauty kind*
> *Loyal and True*
> *Beautiful through and through*
> *Jean that's you 12-9-94*
> *Bob*
> *[with] Happy*
> *Tear*

Here is yet another poem about Mom's self sacrifice. He tells of what he sees are signs of her devotion and love for her family. He "feel [s] and see [s] them every day/Things that you don't say". She attends to her tasks quietly. He reflects on her daily tasks "as I go on my way" and he proceeds to write about what he perceives. And she did do all these things. She was careful and meticulous in her duties. Our house was clean and orderly, our meals delicious. He goes from tasks she does to make our lives pleasant to the more personal aspects of her caregiving-"Self sacrifice and prayers for us/smiles and hugs so fine/Done with eyes that shine/Graceful beauty kind/Loyal and True/Beautiful through and through/Jean that's you". I know she did pray for us all during times of tribulation. She was a wife and mother, after all. But it would have been better if

I had seen the shine in her eyes that Dad saw. He signs off-"Bob/ [with] Happy/Tear"-maybe happy but still a tear.

Maybe [1-8-95]
She and me
Married we be
Me and she
To the other
Other to me
Eyes for none but thee
Oh Queen bee
Only you I see
See you only me
Maybe a score
Left possibly more
Be I with one I adore.
No more.
Bobby
1-8-95

"Maybe" [It may be], the title, sets the stage for this poem. Dad begins by referring to himself in the first person singular objective-"me" and Mom in the third person singular nominative-she, not in the third person singular objective (her) or in the second person singular (you), but "She and me". Why not "she and I" or "you and me"?

Does this suggest that he is familiar with himself but finds her somewhat removed in the context of this poem? "You and me" would seem more intimate in nature between the two and "She and I" would seem more removed emotionally in general. So he starts out talking to himself, not addressing her directly. Then, in the next few lines, he pens-"Married we be/Me and she/To the other/ [and the] Other to me". He could be talking to her directly when he writes-"Married we be" but it becomes apparent he's not when he adds "Me and she". "To the other/ [and the] other to me" also seems impersonal. He doesn't write "to each other" as one might expect. Instead, each is married "to the other" and she is "[the] Other/ [married] to me". Again, he speaks to himself-"me". She seems somehow left out of the equation.

In line six Dad finally addresses her directly-"[I have] Eyes for none but thee" but then proclaims-"Oh Queen bee"-she is supreme among women as the Queen bee is in the hive and only she is really worthy of his attention. However, there had been a time when he did notice others and had involvement with them. Is he trying to reassure her that all this is in the past? Then again, he writes a few more vague lines, similar to the first five of the poem. Lines eight and nine read-"Only you I see/See you only me". Does he mean he sees only her, and he is the only one who understands her-really sees her?-I see only you and only I see you? So, in effect, he may be saying that he only has eyes for her, and that he, and he alone, is the only one who truly knows-"sees"- and understands her. He seems to me lonely in this poem for his sentiment may only be his own, for line nine- "see you only me"- is vague and more likely, due to the word order, favors the interpretation-Only I see you-he is the only one who really sees her-rather than the possibility that he meant- you see only me- which would require the order of words "you" and "see" in the line to be changed. And if so, then he would be telling her that he believes she is exclusive in her love for him.

The focus changes in the last four lines-"Maybe a score/left possibly more"-He was sixty-nine years of age when he wrote this poem, so he predicts they have another ten years or so of life left. During this time-"Be I with [I will be] with the one I adore/ no more". "No more" could mean he will have no more than his devotion to her as he may not have any assurance that he has her devotion. There is also an implication of his own mortality/ annihilation-He will be with her for another score or so, but maybe nevermore.

Dove [Feb. 9th 1995]
Helped me up when I was   <u>*To Jean*</u>
Nothing.
Never let me down
Kind dove cooing each time
I am around.
Laughed and cried together
With children we are bound
Decade after decade to become
More tightly wound
Passing toward eternity
Some peace we have
Found
[with] Love and Trust
Bob Feb. 9th 1995

This poem seems to acknowledge a mutual affection and love, in some contrast to the last poem. Dad focuses on ways she has uplifted him and supported him throughout their relationship-"Helped me up when I was/Nothing". Dad always carried insecurity and feelings of worthlessness due to his immigrant background. He appeared more than confident on the outside but underneath is where he felt his insecurity. Maybe Mom's support is what changed his opinion of himself as time went on and maybe she improved his status in his mind simply because of his association with her. It also seems he is recognizing her intentional effort to be emotionally supportive of him in the following line-"Never let me down". Next, he describes how she was this way-"Kind dove cooing each time I am around"- she brings him up with her kindness towards him. He may use the word "dove" to describe her and their relationship, as doves are known to be affectionate and mate for life.

Next, he summarizes the significant aspects of their relationship- "Laughed and cried together/With children we are bound"-there is emotional intimacy and responsibility that cements their union. He adds-"Decade after decade to become/More tightly wound"-which is reminiscent of a watch (time) that, on some level, is at its maximum capacity, maybe a threat of breakage for whatever reason. But then in the last line-"Passing toward eternity/Some peace we have/ Found." He sees their corporeal end in sight, so maybe they will be able to stick it out. He also tells the reader here that they have come to a sort of peace in their advancing years and maybe in anticipation of an eternity together, as he has mentioned in numerous of his poems.

Wishing Well [5-16-95]
Love to see you happy
Hate to see you sad.
Your body is still firm
With shoulders so square
Back upright and not round

Still solid to caress.
Appetite is usually dandy
Coctail [Cocktail] partner super handy
Thoughtful generous and kind
Oh! Woman super fine
Delivers love sublime
I will be foreever [forever] thyne [thine]
If my wish upon a star
Please miracle cure appear
For the one I hold dear
So I would never need
another tear
And pain never more to feel.
So carefree we would be
Me and thee.
Discomfort free
Bobby 5-16-95

This poem starts out on a positive note and with compliments of Mom's physical and personal attributes. But first, Dad makes a contrast of her moods that affect him-"Love to see you happy/Hate to see you sad"-his following compliments, presumably to lift her mood to the happy side. His description of her in the following nine lines focus on her physical attributes, soft manner and sensuality that are pleasing to him in an erotic manner. Next, he moved on to the nature of their relationship-He pledges his loyalty-"I will be forever thine [yours]". Finally, he moves again, as in other of his poems, to his concern for her wellbeing-"If my wish upon a star [he beckons the universe]/please miracle cure appear/for the one I hold dear". Next, he describes the effect her state has on him-"So [then] I would never need/another tear". The outcome of her emotional freedom would be for both-"...pain never more to feel./So carefree we would be /Me and thee/Discomfort free".

See [3-31-96]
We eat together
Both grow older
And less bold
Nevertheless
Am most in bliss
When we are not amiss
But in mutual bliss
Like Sunday A.M. s
At breakfast time
3-31-96 Cheers or Ciao
Zivjo too.
Bobby Love
You

This poem may have been written while Mom and Dad vacationed on the QE2, or at least he uses the cruise line's stationary, the emblem on the top right of the page, Queen Elizabeth 2 and the word CUNARD on the bottom center. The title "See" is indicative of his insight expressed in the poem of their evolving relationship in their waning years-"We eat together/Both grow older/And less bold". He recognizes their decline. Then, in contrast, -"Nevertheless/[I] Am most in bliss/When we are not amiss/But in mutual bliss/Like Sunday A.M. s/At breakfast time"-the simple pleasures they share are the most cherished by him. They would go to their favorite spot every Sunday for brunch at the River House Resort. A couple martinis or Bloody Mary's were always a part of this two or so hour outing. He signs off in an interesting manner-"Cheers or Ciao/Zivjo too"-Cheers in English, Ciao in Italian, and Zivjo in Slovenian, loosely translated-To the Good Life"-these are the languages he knew. He ends with-"Bobby Love/You".

Forlorn [no date other than 1995 on QE2 stationary]
Who [and] what was this man so tall and stately.
Now bent, thin, frail, gray [,] yet quiet [-] grandly.
Time brings this heritage inately [innately].
Hands now thin wan tremble sadly.
At mass he stands bowed now humbly
Praying waiting for a death that ['] s timely
Nothing more revently [reverently/revenant or] sublimely.

Dad writes this poem on QE2 stationary too. He may have written this poem on the ship or later, at home. It has a rather dark feel to it. He starts out asking himself a question-"Who [and] what was this man so tall and stately". Was he peering at a photo of himself long ago or was this picture merely in his mind? And where did this man go, he wants to know. He contrasts this man he knew with the current man-"Now bent, thin, frail, gray yet quiet grandly". Grand is (#125, pg. 629, 8. [Colloq.], admirable; delightful; SYN.-grand is applied to that which makes a strong impression because of its…dignity…). I'd like to comment here on the last two words of this second line-"yet quiet grandly". The positive aspect of his aging is his mellowing and insight. He speaks less and listens more. He is more humble than his youthful form. He explains the natural progression in life-"Time brings this heritage innately". The word "innately" suggests that his wisdom comes with the aging process just as humility does. He has become a sage-(#126, pg. 1284, 1. a very wise old man. 2. a man... venerated and respected for his wisdom, experience, and judgment).

He returns to his physical condition-"Hands now thin [and] wan [,] tremble sadly". I remember this gradual transformation of his. He developed a tremor that compromised his independence and, within a few years of this poem being written, his writing ceased. Again, in line five, he returns to the psychological changes that are the result of his physical decline. He speaks as though he is merely an observer of himself with the use of the word "he" rather than I-"At mass he stands bowed now humbly"-it is almost as though he is already in some other realm of the departed who have arrived at a spirituality not possible in a corporeal state, and here he is at the Catholic mass with spirituality all around him. Next, he writes-"Praying waiting for a death that's timely"-he is ready to die and maybe even one foot into the grave. He prays and waits for his release and hopes it will be "timely"-that he won't linger too long. His last is-"Nothing more revently sublimely". I think he combined two different words when he wrote "revently"-reverently and revenant. He feels reverence for his creator-beholden to this grantor of his wish to be free. Revenant is (#127, pg. 1245, 1. a person who returns, as after a long absence. 2. a person who returns as a spirit, after death; ghost)-both seem to apply in the context, for he will be returning to his maker and will enter into the spiritual realm. He uses the word "sublimely' to describe the emotion he will feel upon this happening. Sublime is (#128, pg.

1452, 3. [Poetic] elated; joyful). It would take almost seventeen years before his prayer was answered.

Sweet Sorrow Me Amie [95- to 4-8-96]
Part each A.M. [,] go around
At times things get me down
No longer a carefree boy.
Treating worries like a toy.
Problems now are everywhere
Shaking them off is not simple fare.
Ah! But soon we won't be there
I know that you must see
How sweetly I think of Thee
Together we seem to be mainly
In each others proximity
If I am gone your form
From my mind is never gone.
Actually here with you I
would rather be.
That's why the plans I make
Usually we together take
So new conversations,
We may more easily prate
Without you Trips for me
are hard to make.
Because my heart I must
partially forsake
Pardon my darker moods
My Trips to outer space
I am not perfect you see

So my love for you is
not free
It comes with a penalty
The penalty is me
Bobby
95- to 4-8-96

This is another of Dad's darker poems that became more prevalent in these waning years of his. In his first line-"Part each A.M. go around"-I think he speaks of his habit of taking walks by himself. Mom was never a walker unless he coaxed her into it when they traveled together, especially to explore any of the cities they frequented. Anyway, in this poem, he doesn't seem particularly enthused about his solitary A.M. walk. While he walks he thinks about stuff, this time, "At times things get me down". He is "No longer a carefree boy"-and he had been one in many ways. I remember him being so in his twenties when I was a child, and even on into his mid-thirties and beyond. But life caught up with him and now he is already feeling the manifestations of a dement-ing illness. So he begins "Treating worries like a toy"-he is somewhere between a competent man and a person involved in the reversal of time, so his worries become like the pastime of a child with his toys. He goes on-"Problems now are everywhere/ Shaking them off is not simple fare"-he becomes preoccupied with his newfound struggle. Next, he has a revelation-"Ah! but soon we won't be there"-Where? Does he mean they won't be in a worried state or that they won't be around at all? If he means they won't be around at all, and if he is suggesting that "soon" they won't be there (somewhere that someone isn't), then this implies that, on some level, they have already departed. If he had written "soon we won't be here (somewhere that someone is)", that would have meant that they would soon be departing from their current location or situation. If he means they won't continue on in a worried state, then maybe he thinks they'll both be so addled, nothing will bother them.

In line eight, the tone of this poem changes abruptly. Now he looks to a more positive view of their future, with a focus on the present and small pleasures they can still enjoy together. He pens-"I know that you must see/How sweetly I think of thee"- and in the next several lines he describes how her presence is such a comfort to him. "Together we seem to be mainly/in each other's proximity/If I am gone your form/From my mind is never gone/ Actually here with you I /would rather be/That's why the plans I make/Usually we together take./So new conversations,/We may more easily prate/". Prate is (#129, pg. 1147, to talk much and foolishly; chatter). They are together so much now that there might not be so much to say to each other, other than idle chatter. He goes on-"Without you Trips for me/are hard to make/Because my heart I must forsake/"-[when not in your presence]. Of course, he always missed her every time they were apart, not just in their older years, and this is evident in many of his poems.

Then again, the tone of this poem shifts to an apology for his nature-"Pardon my darker moods/My trips to outer space/I am not perfect you see/ So my love for you is/not free/It comes with a penalty/The penalty is me". I remember his "darker moods" and his "trips to outer space". He suffered fits of melancholy and irritability from his thirties on, but then would recover and be his exuberant self again. His "trips to outer space" were long-standing too-another term-"absent-minded"-comes to my mind in more ways than one. He knew he wasn't always the easiest person to live with, and in his later years he tried to tone himself down. Sometimes he was successful. So here, he apologizes (to the person who always meant the most to him) for his foibles, because his intention is never to harm her.

It must have taken a while for him to work on and complete this poem-starting some time in 1995 and finishing April 8th, 1996. I also note that he scribbled out a word or name below his "Bobby". It's hard to make out-but possibly "truly" as an adjunct to his name.

A Day [12-8-96]
Sunny A.M. on Baptism Day
As Todd and Liz spend
A morning at play
Breakfast served in a leisurely way.
Todd & Doug go out to play
While Jean puts dishes away
Everyone scrubbed [,] Then in
Finery dressed
Out to the chapel we trek
As all the others are met.
Ceremony follows as the proper
Words the principles [principals] say.
With water draining all sins away
Peacefully re-congregate on 9th St.
Before we all meet again to eat
The lunch was jolly and long

With wine food and good cheer
No arguements [arguments] here
Every one departs & Travels back
Good luck as all return home
To end an unforgettable Day
Rough draft
Forgotten & Rediscovered
12-8-96-
Bobby
Did not show
Jean because of the corrections

In this poem Dad writes about one of his grandchildren's baptism day-Elizabeth, my sister Nora and her husband Todd's eldest daughter. Dad describes a "Sunny A.M. for Baptism Day/ As Todd and Liz spend/a morning at play". The rest of the poem describes the pomp and circumstance, a somber event at the church, when this infant is blessed with holy water to "drain away all sin"-which I suppose will last her lifetime. The chapel event over, family congregates at Mom and Dad's home on 9th Street- "The lunch was jolly and long/With wine food and good cheer" (what about song?) and "No arguments here". Finally, "everyone departs [,] Travels back" and then "Good luck as all return home/ To end an unforgettable Day". Dad writes a note with a different pen underneath this saga, but it is difficult to decipher. The gist of it, anyway, is that he had some cross-outs so labeled this attempt a rough draft. Then he writes-"Forgotten & Rediscovered" and "Did not show /Jean because of the corrections" Whether or not he ever wrote a revision, I don't know. If he did, it wasn't in the album.

However, this unrevised version was. I suspect then, that Mom did see this one. I believe he wrote this poem mostly for Mom because after her conversion from Lutheranism to Catholicism she became fanatical. I believe she felt guilt for having forsaken her family's faith with her conversion and kept this secret from her parents forever. I also think Dad wrote this poem because he loved family events. They didn't always go as smoothly as this one, so his comment about "good cheer" and "no arguments" suggests that he was pleased that it went so well.

Remember [8-27-97]
I Remember how when [we] were more carefree
Your eyes would shine when you looked at me
And mine, I am sure, would shine back to thee
Recalling too how beautiful you seemed to be
Your form so perfect [,] your face pristine
In elderly years, altered by time
Your beauty of body mind and soul
Remain unbelievably fine
Still flawless in my mind totaly [totally] sublime
Approaching the end of the line [,] recall our time
I hope with some peace and pleasure in mind.
Bobby,
8-27-97
P.S. Maybe we could replay just one time.
On the Queen Elizabeth line in the some time.
Or maybe drop a dime on the S.S.T. line.

Dad writes here again on the QE2 stationary. These poems may have be written during their cruise or later on with some saved, as dad always collected mementos and sundries on each travel adventure he went on-hotel soaps, complimentary shampoo, plastic shower caps, breakfast jelly samples, bread sticks, swizzle sticks-anything not nailed down and not too valuable. I think this habit had something to do with his childhood during the Great Depression.

He starts out reminiscing-"I remember how when [we] were more carefree/Your eyes would shine when you looked at me". He recognizes that the shine in her eyes was her adoration of him, but this only seemed to happen while they were "more carefree". He also seems unsure about his own reaction to her gaze-"And mine, I am sure, would shine back to thee". But his adding "I am sure" really seems to suggest that maybe he isn't sure, he only imagines that is what his response would have been.

In the fourth line he continues to reminisce, but his musings now focus on her physical beauty-"Recalling too how beautiful you seemed to be"-again, his "seeming to be" suggests he only imagines how he must have felt. He almost questions his own ability to assess his memories accurately. He elaborates-"Your form so perfect [,] your face pristine". Pristine is (#130, pg. 1159, 1. characteristic of the earliest, or an earlier, period or condition; original. 2. still pure or untouched; uncorrupted; unspoiled)-he remembers a more innocent time in their lives and it also seems he alludes to something deeper than just her physical beauty. Next, he fast forwards to the present-"In elderly years, altered by time/Your beauty of body mind and soul/Remain unbelievable fine". She is "Still flawless" in his mind, and all this makes him feel "sublime". Finally, he tells her that they are "Approaching the end of the line" and he hopes she, too, will be able to recall their time together with "peace and pleasure in [her] mind" as he is able to do.

After he signs off-"Bobby" with the date-8-27-97-he writes a postscript-"Maybe we could replay just one time/On the Queen Elizabeth line in the some time/Or maybe drop a dime on the S.S.T. line". He hopes they will still have a chance of taking another cruise together before the end. When he writes "in the some time" I wonder if this thought might include not only some time in their future lives together, but also a possibility for them to take this trip even after their deaths and in another realm-"[in the] some time"-or not in time.

Love you Jean [11-23-97]

Love you Jean

Yes I do

Composing as I sit

In my own Pew

You're the best

Better than the rest.

The things you do

Are good all through

So you see I love you

Bobby

11-23-97

The above is only for your eyes

I almost feel guilty presenting this poem for Dad ends the poems with "The above is only for your eyes". But they are no longer on this earth, floating in another sphere, so I doubt they will object to my sharing Dad's sentiment with whoever might be interested. He starts out-"Love you Jean/Yes I do"-The "Yes I do" a form of superlative and confirmation of his feelings for her. Next- "Composing as I sit/in my own Pew"-he pens this while attending mass. Dad was always distracted and bored in church. He'd drift off with his head bobbing up and down as he took a snooze. Or he'd goof off, sometimes entertaining young kids in the pew ahead of him by making goofy faces at them. This time, he decides to write this poem to Mom. The poem is light and playful-"You [']re the best/ Better than the rest/The things you do/are good all through" and he ends with "So you see I love you"-an attempt to convince her of his devotion.

Etherial [Ethereal] [2-23-98]

A human angles [angel's] touch I feel

Weather [Whether] you are far or near

When your [you're] near your touch is real

When far it [']s just as dear

Because I experience the

etherial [ethereal]

Love ya

Bobbie

2-23-98

Dad has his tendency to misspell words in his poems and this one is no exception. As time went by, it became more prevalent. I suspect it was the beginning of symptoms of his dementia. At any rate, he maintained his ability to relate an emotion or thought, and in many respects, his poetry evolved into a more tender, thoughtful and spiritual rendering. He begins this poem telling the reader that he feels her "angel's touch" all around him,-her essence, her spirit-no matter where she is and this is because he "experience [s] the/ [ethereal]-a connection with the un-corporeal. This theme of their souls goes right back to my favorite-"Again-Again"-written during the advent of their relationship. Again, ethereal is (#131, pg. 499, 3. heavenly; celestial; not earthly) and celestial is (#132, pg. 235, 2. of heaven; heavenly; divine). He signs off-"Love ya/ Bobbie". What's with the "ya"?

> *Reverberations [6-4-98]*
> *A dark area in her head*
> *Reverberations incesently [incessantly]*
> *Carooms [carom] inside her mind.*
> *Bounding side to side*
> *For decades rickoshaying [ricocheting]*
> *Ceasing not from year to year*
> *One after the other*
> *Nothing stops the melody*
> *But don ['] t you see as*
> *you pray to God daily*
> *Reason begs reality*
> *Realize even grave*
> *sinners from above -*
> *after a few words or so*   *over→*
> *All recieve [receive] absolution*
> *But not you.*
> *Why not Why not*
> *You have earned peace.*
> *Forgive yourself*
> *God has more than*

10,000 Times
and I haven't
because I don't
think you have done
wrong.
Bobby 6-4-98

Dad starts this poem on the back of the Beverly Hilton Hotel stationary and uses the side with the logo for his postscript. The title provides the subject matter of his poem-one of his darker and more desperate of his commentary. It all happens in "A dark area in her head/Reverberations incessantly/carom/ inside her mind/bounding side to side/For decades ricocheting/ceasing not from year to year/ One after the other/Nothing stops the melody" Reverberate is (#133, pg. 1246, 1. to throw back (sound); cause a sound to re-echo). Incessant is (#134, pg. 735, not stopping; never ceasing; continuing or being repeated without interruption; constant). Carom is (#135, pg. 223, 3. a hitting and rebounding). Ricochet is (#136, pg. 1252, the motion made by an object that rebounds or skips one or more times). And all this motion is "Ceasing not from year to year/One after the other/ [and] Nothing stops the melody [of this dance]. Dad seems exacerbated with this redundant mind set of hers. He creates a visual, kinetic description of her mental anguish. The words-reverberations, incessant, carom, bounding, ricocheting, ceasing not, melody-all combine to form a depiction of an active, ever-moving and present, self-inflicted torment.

In the next portion of the poem he attempts to persuade her to rid herself of this constant preoccupation with guilt. He tells her-"But don't you see as/you pray to God daily/Reason begs reality". Beg can be (#137, pg., 133, 1. to use an argument that assumes as proved the very thing one is trying to prove. 2. loosely, to evade the issue). So he tries to tell her that reason proves his point and adheres to reality. He elaborates on this notion-" Realize even grave/sinners from above/after a few words or so/All receive absolution"-trying to convince her to change her tune. He continues to plead his case-"But not you/Why not Why not/You have earned peace".

Dad adds the underlined word "over" with an arrow above the word, directing the reader to turn the page over to the front page of the stationary. Here is where he makes a plea-"Forgive yourself/God has more than 10,000 Times", but it would be only after her mind went adrift that she would forget self-perceived offenses that fueled her unrelenting guilt. Next, he tells her-"...I haven't [forgiven you]/because I don't/think you have done wrong" Again, he attempts to convince her that her thinking is in error.

To Me [8-15-98]
So sweet to me you seem
That at times I feast my eyes
And they shed Tears of Joy
At the corners of my nose
as they trickle to my lips
with saltyness [saltiness] so sweet
Then with a short breath or Two
a gentle chest Tightness grows
Then again I return to reality
Because you are still next to me
Filling the air with extacy [ecstasy]
for me.

Bobby 8-15-98
Buckle up relax.
Love ya still but deep.

This poem has tones of sentiment and melancholy as Dad describes his silent gaze that creates an emotional and sensual response to the sight of his beloved. The sight that inspired him becomes secondary to his facial sensations-"So sweet to me you seem/That at times I feast my eyes/And they shed Tears of Joy/At the corners of my nose/as they trickle down to my lips/with saltiness so sweet". The sensation that encompasses his whole face seems to lead him to a trance-like state that is broken only by what he describes in the next few lines-"Then with a short breath or Two/a gentle chest Tightness grows" and again he becomes aware of his surroundings-"Then again I return to reality/Because you are still next to me/Filling the air with ecstasy/for me"-his focus goes back to the source of his emotional pleasure.

After he signs off with his name and the date the poem was written, he adds-"Buckle up relax/Love ya still but deep". I'm not sure about the "ya" which just might diminish his proclamation a bit. Yet, it seems he is trying to reassure her about his devotion with the rest of the message that tells her he still loves her and that his love is "deep". The "Buckle up" may be a reference to the wild side of their relationship that he promoted and that Mom usually went along with.

Ivory [11-10-98]
Like Carved Ivory
and as pure of mind
thoughtful and Kind

Eyes that can shine
Jean forever mine Bobby
11-10-98

Mom had an ivory skin tone that Dad adored. In his mind, her fair skin mirrored her gentle nature. I suspect he chose her, in part, due to the contrast of her ivory complexion to his olive complexion-at a time not considered politically correct-and maybe to instill in his offspring a more acceptable appearance in his new country. He goes on-"and as pure of mind/thoughtful and Kind/"-he attributes an ivory complexion to purity, thoughtfulness and kindness, not the way he would describe himself. Finally, he writes of her "Eyes that can shine"-maybe another of her attributes that suggest purity of spirit. He will reap the benefit, again, in his association with her, expressed in the last line-"Jean forever mine".

I Love Jean [12-11-98]
I Love Jean from top
to bottom.
My mind and heart
she had gotten.
Bobby
12-11-98

This ditty was written on a small card, possibly accompanied by a bouquet of flowers or some other gift. A little heart is drawn above the word "heart" as a form of exclamation point. The sentiment, like the heart, is playful. He uses "she" (third person) rather than you (second person) which leads the reader to the conclusion that he writes this to himself. He still signs the card "Bobby" suggesting the message is meant for her eyes too.

Jean [1-10-99]

My dearest being.

Fragile as a butterfly.

Sweet as nectar pie.

Not unlike a dove,

Docile and full of love.

Don ['] t cry dear thing.

You are a fine human being.

Too soft is your heart.

Untill [Until] death you depart.

Inner peace for you I pray.

Hope you find same one day.

Soon

1-10-99

Bobby is still

In love [with] you

Dad describes Mom in this poem as the epitome of femaleness-"Fragile", "Sweet", dove-like, "Docile", "full of love", "soft". He thinks she is so sensitive that it is a detriment to her so he tries to bolster her confidence-"You are a fine human being", and "My dearest being". With the line-"Until death you depart"-he suggests that death may be her only release from her condition. He hopes it won't come to that, but that she will find "inner peace" while still here on earth. This poem, again, uncovers the effect her emotional state has on him-a torment that he will eventually inherit. He signs off-"Bobby is still/in love with you" to reassure her that she can count on him.

Poems [7-13-1999]

Some are about love
Others cite beauty
Again there is duty
Or
Possibly all the above
Ode to one ['] s loyal wife
Standing by through strife
Which I hold so dear
That death I need not fear
For tranquility is near
How fine it ['] s been
Fulfilled completely
As I am.
Bobby
7-13-1999

Dad starts out this poem commenting on poetry itself-its subject matter and its reason for being. Love and beauty are surely common topics but he adds duty to the list. Perhaps duty alludes to the poet's role in bringing his or her readers to some deeper understanding or redemption, to help make the world just a little bit better. In his case, it seems his focus in numerous of his poems is to free his wife of her torment, to have her see the light. He elaborates in the next few lines. His poem is an "Ode to ones loyal wife/Standing by through strife/which I hold so dear"-and she did stand by him in this manner. Because of his trust in her love, he isn't afraid of anything-even death-"that death I need not fear". He describes how death will be-"For tranquility is near". And finally, he relishes in their lives together-"How fine it's been/Fulfilled completely/As I am"-and he owes it all to her.

Also [10-31-99] [written on Halloween]
Older now it ['] s clear
also
Time together is more dear
also
Because we grew so near
also
Easier now to melancholy Tears
also
Love you more it seems to appear.
Also
No more do I fear
Love
Bobby
10-31-99
10 D.S.T.

This poem is similar to the last in sentiment and subject matter. It is written three and a half months later. Maybe that's why Dad titles the poem "Also". "Older now it's clear"-there is wisdom here. Then, "Time together is more dear"-for there is more awareness of the finite nature of life that comes with age, unlike the illusion of being omnipotent, as youth often consider themselves to be. Their relationship is also enhanced "because we grew so near". Each thought is followed by "also" to connect the relationship of one line to the other, so because of the significance of their being so near (and dear), he is "easier to melancholy tears". And because of how important she had become to him, he is more aware that he must "Love [her] more it seems to appear". Finally, this leads to his observation that "No more do I fear". This line is similar to the conclusion of the previous poem-"Poems"-a fulfillment in life due to his most significant relationship, an enhanced sentimentality, and a tranquil acceptance of whatever else occurs. I don't know what the significance of "10 D.S.T." is beneath his name and date of the poem.

> *Too Late [2-26-00]*
> *Right or wrong It*
> *Shouldn't be*
> *That anything comes*
> *between you and me.*
> *My sorrow is deep*
> *and married to my mind*
> *Like other similar times*
> *Deeply etched*
> *Painfully clear*
> *Pardon me*
> *Oh one that*
> *I hold so dear*
> *Sealed with a Tear Bobby*
> *2-26-00*

In this desolate poem, Dad laments the state of his relationship with Mom. It is unmentioned what transpired or what his transgression is this time-"Right or wrong It/Shouldn't be/That anything comes/ between you and me". But something has, for he states next-"My sorrow is deep/and married to my mind/Like other similar times/Deeply etched/Painfully clear"-his sorrow is "married" to his mind, "deeply etched", "painfully clear"-an assault to his soul. Dad often spoke up without thinking first and this is what usually got him in trouble. And then Mom was sensitive and could hold a grudge indefinitely, so there it is-the recurring predicament. Again, he asks for her forgiveness-"Pardon me/ Oh one that/ I hold so dear/Sealed with a Tear". Bobby/2-26-00.

Older Now [7-6-00]
The 70dies are here
and we are still near.
I am more quiet now
Don ['] t say love you enough
Even though it ['] s not tough.
Think of your eyes when we wed
Nothing needs To be said
Dimmer now because of pain
I consider that a shame
& Hope I am not to blaim [blame]
And
As I sit with a heavy chest
Will try my very best
To show more Interest
and give my ass less rest
Bobbie
7-6-00

This is one of the last poems in the album-his cursive is quavery-a sign of not good things to come. His words are a rather sad rendering. He starts-"The 70dies are here", and the end result-

"dies". I suspect this was intentional on his part. Das was about to be 74 and Mom 72 and "they are still near [each other]". Next, he comments on the changes age has brought to him-"I am more quiet now/Don't say love you enough" and then his mind brings back earlier times-"Think of your eyes when we wed" and they are "Dimmer now because of pain" which he considers "a shame" and he hopes he's not to blame. I don't think she was the only one who lost the gleam in the eyes. He, too became burdened with a kind of apathy as time went by. In the last four lines he tells her he will try his best to be more attentive, but he has this disease of the brain that will squelch any efforts of his to follow through with his good intentions.

Happy Birthday [7-18-00]
Scotch Party Today
Law & Order to Play
If it ['] s recorded Okay
But I also must say
Love you the same way
as yesterday
Bobby 7-18-00

This ditty was written on a Happy Birthday card on Mom's birthday, probably accompanied by flowers that are illustrated on the card. It was written shortly after the last poem. This one seems more upbeat. Dad liked to have scotch parties and often invited a few extra couples, interested in partaking, for these events. The scotch at these gatherings was accompanied by complementary fare. The focus was to enjoy this delectable elixir-at least that's what he thought it was. I attended a few of these get-togethers myself.

I suspect the two would be all that would participate in the scotch event on this occasion, for there also seemed to be plans to watch "Law and Order" while they sipped on their drinks-"Law & Order to Play/If it ['] s recorded Okay". Dad had, by this time, taken to taping all sorts of shows on television, then carefully labeling, with great detail, the contents of each and every tape. I think I still have a few somewhere, but of course, technology has long since made his creations obsolete. Then his-"If it ['] s recorded Okay"-meaning one never knew if anything or the right thing would show up on any given tape Dad had anything to do with. Finally, he changes course again, and tells her how much he loves her on her special day-"But I also must say/Love you the same way/as yesterday". I'm sure this little poem was his unwrapped birthday gift.

Just Because [no date]
I love you
Simple as that. Bobby.
This is a card from Autry's 4 Seasons Florist. It has no date.
Pray [10-20-00]
My love you see
Is so dear to me
She is not pain free
Hurts are too many
But her heart a plenty
When happy her glow
Her eyes do it show
Then happyness [happiness] is mine
But when she is down
In tears my eyes drown

And in my glum
Fearing what is to come.
Pray! 10-20-00
Bobby

This is the last poem in the album collection. If there were others written then it seems they must be lost forever. The year 2000 was a turning point for my parents. They had purchased a condo in Vancouver, Washington first and traveled back and forth between home and Vancouver. In 2000, they sold our family home and purchased another condo on the river in Bend. This is about the time Dad seemed to become more frail. He would forget and developed a tremor-apparent in some of his later poetic cursive. He would finally lose his ability to speak anything but a few tremulous words. Here is his last known poem.

"My love you see/Is so dear to me". The poem seems to be an intimate prayer to God. In these first few lines he wants to explain how important his wife is to him. Then he proceeds to describe her complicated mood swings-the light and the dark-"She is not pain free/ Hurts are too many/ But her heart a plenty/When happy her glow/ Her eyes do it show" and then the happiness is his. "But when she is down/In tears my eyes drown/And in my glum/Fearing what is to come/Pray!"-While in his "glum" he imagines the worst. He always was good at prediction. And, finally, with his recognition of an onerous future, all he can do now is "Pray [tell]"-What is ahead of us. He is entreating God to let him see the future and maybe even intervene on their behalf. It didn't seem his prayers were answered.

Guestbook Beach Retreat Poems

Dad discovered our beach place while running along the shore one morning in the summer of 1972. He noticed it high up on a cliff and jogged up to inspect his find. He talked to the folks who had converted two homes into one condominium. They gave him a tour and a brochure. He returned to the place we had been to before this find, and exclaimed that with our next visit to the coast, we would spend it elsewhere. This new spot was covered in toll painting and the apartments divided up to make eight altogether. I feel Dad's presence with each word I read and with each word I write- reliving our time together. Every time I visit our beach spot I read Dad's entries in these guest journals, take in the aura and serenity of the place and feel his presence, maybe even more than while he was on this earth, and my own memories of time spent in this special place come alive.

#1 Penthouse Puzzling Sea October 6-7-1972

Penthouse puzzling sea

Forever etched in our memory.

Frank-Jean-Doug-Nora

Mom and Dad's first visit was in October 6-7 of 1972, just a few months after his find. Doug and Nora were still living at home. He writes the ages of each family member on this getaway underneath the names of each-46,44,14,5. The word puzzling is curious-One definition is (#138, pg. 470, [ACD], to require much mental effort)-maybe even engendering awe, which will "forever

[be] etched in our [their] memory" That was all he needed to say about the scene right outside his beach-front abode.

#2 Sunset Shining Moon Dec. 7th 8-9 too 1972

Sunset shining moon scimitar

Above the southern horizon

Two leagues below a solitary star

Mark an established high

Record low outside buffered by

A five log fire [,] brandy [,] coffee

A rarity; indeed a coast full of snow

At zero and below.

Once but nare [never] again will we

See it so. (from the Penthouse) scimitar/simitar/symitar? SP/No Webster/[unintelligible]

Frank & Jean Kerkoch

Bend, Oregon.

Mom and Dad had their second stay (#2) at the beach place-[it seems w/o kids]. Dad describes the beauty that surrounds them. The "moon scimitar" (the preferred spelling for scimitar) refers to the curved crescent shape of the moon that night. Scimitar is (footnote #139, pg. 1305, a short curved sword with an edge on the convex side). This is how he describes this moon at sunset. The moon shines "Above the southern horizon/"Two leagues below a solitary star" A league is (footnote #140, pg. 831, a measure of distance)-here, between the star above and the moon below. In the next two lines I believe he is suggesting that this sight he observes is marking a "high/Record low outside [temperature for the Oregon coast] which is "buffered by/A five log fire, brandy, coffee". Buffer is (footnote # 141, pg. 190, to lessen or absorb the shock of collision or impact), so the fire, brandy and coffee will buffer the cold. He goes on to explain to the reader that the snow-covered beach is "A rarity; indeed a coast full of snow/At zero and below". He predicts that this sort of happening is so rare, it is likely nare [never] to be seen again by them. He signs off with both their names and home town. He writes a comment to the right of the main body of the poem-his wondering about the proper spelling of the word scimitar. The first is correct and preferred, the second legitimate but less prevalent, and the third is incorrect. He notes that without his Webster's dictionary, he is at a disadvantage. The word underneath "Webster" is unintelligible. Dad talked to family and friends many times over about their witnessing snow on the beach-quite a rare occasion. Whether or not they ever witnessed this phenomenon again isn't known to me. In the left margin he pens a big #2 and a drawing of a wine bottle. In the right margin he penned the word "moon", crossed it out, and instead drew a star with a moon underneath to mimic the first three lines of the poem. I guess he thought the word wouldn't represent the portrayal in the poem as well as a drawing.

Met with the Bunch/11-16-17-18-1973 #3 visit
Set up in the Penthouse along with the eights
Were told there was a big Gale on the way
Topped the big keg—Drank
Toasting ourselves and the big one above
Lost the femmes early [,] another at two but
The big "L's stayed up till four
Enjoying pore after pore

Crippled by quenched thirst awoke at mid A.M.
Was sunny and bright
The Gale didn't show
So hit a peaceful beach under the blue.
It's strength thundered though
Detoxified refreshed restored
Toast to Lynn. Frank & Jean Kerkoch

This was the first time I was included in a trip to what had become our beach place. I was a few months pregnant with my firstborn but just didn't know it yet. So Dad tells the reader that they "met the bunch" from the south and east of Oregon for this gathering. It seems Mom and Dad were in the Penthouse and the rest of us were in unit 8. They were told there would be "a big Gale [storm] on the way" but some of the group decided to party anyway. They "tapped the big keg-Drank/[then proceeded to] Toasting ourselves and the big one above"-their creator. The hard core partiers "Lost the femmes early [and] another [bunch] at two [A.M. gave up too] but/The big "L's" stayed up till four/enjoying pour after pour". The two L's were my ex Leo and Lynn-the son of the folks who owned the Penthouse-hard-core partiers for sure. The result-"crippled by quenched thirst awoke at mid A.M." But then it "Was sunny and bright/[and] The Gale didn't show [after all]/So [everyone] hit a peaceful beach under the blue [sky]. Finally, he writes- "It ['] s [the tide's] strength [that]/thundered through/[and]detoxified [,] refreshed [, and] restored [all who needed such]". On the bottom left Dad pens "Toast to Lynn" with a drawing which might suggest a keg and a glass of beer.

[With] Nora Too-Nov. 27-28-29-30 [1975] [stay #4] Ersatz-Frank and Jean in #8

[with] Nora too-Came in the sun
Left in the rain. Hell of a Holiday
Gone again. K-75
No time to
Pen my usual refrain.

This poem was written during their forth visit-#4 Erzatz-[I believe is visit in Slovenian]. This time Nora was there with them-hence-"[with] Nora too"-She was 5 years old in 1975 and the only one left at home of the four of us kids. Maybe they were so busy entertaining her that Dad didn't have a lot of time to wax poetic-but Dad was able to express some melancholy upon his departure-"a holiday/gone again" —maybe reflection upon that inevitable final visit one can't predict that leads to the grave.

At Times October 7-8-9. [stay] #5 –
At times we can't get the penthouse for 2 or 4 [inhabitants]
so we axcept [accept] something on another floor & still
find pleasure galore—
October 7th —sunny out (unheard of) 85° with a 5 mile breeze
Stay [in] #4 through a newly painted penthouse door
Hail to you we decree the empty wine
bottles you see including
Rich & Bourg #5988
Anniz 1962 (Bellecthan '63)
We take the memory-Oh Ted & Vann
if Lynn is back let us know if you
want to sell a slice of the pie

to an old couple with their hearts in pent-sky.
Kerkoch 76 Bend, Or.

In this poem Dad laments not being able to get into his favorite unit-The Penthouse/# 7. As he has mentioned in the past, it hasn't always been available, and so he "axcepts [accepts] something on another floor & still/finds pleasure galore—". The weather is exceptional-October 7th with its 85 degrees and a mild breeze. Their stay this time is in #4 at the interior of the building. I suspect that in lines six through nine he lets the owners know that he leaves a few choice empty bottles of wine he and Mom enjoyed together as a token of their appreciation. He then addresses the owners of the penthouse by name-Ted and Vann-letting them know that they will take the memory of the stay with them. Lynn is Ted and Vann's son who might weigh in about Dad's idea to buy into the place. Dad asks if they might consider a partial [or maybe complete] purchase of their favorite unit-The Penthouse-and refers to himself and Mom as "an old couple with their hearts in pent-sky." I don't know if they ever heard back but nothing of this sort ever took place, not that Dad didn't continue to dream of owning one of the units-especially his favorite-The Penthouse. He draws what I think is a cigar that he labels as "corny", I think with drawing of a bottle of wine next to it and to accompany it.

Tide Out Feb 7-9:00 P.M.
Alone than [then?] three descend
One hundred steps to a
night time quiet beach.
Above two stars shine through
Thin whisps [wisps/whispers] of air suspended dew

Cheryl Krkoč

Along are lights up on the hills
Both filtered through trees and dew
50 [degrees] –No wind at all
Ocean ['] s white cresting waves-move
Four –five at a time ever smaller
Towards shore while up on the hill
Smoke columns move straight up
Are they
Fingers of praise to one above. K-77
Penthouse #5 stay.

This poem describes the serene beauty of the coastline. The sensual flavor of this poem is predominant and, at the end, he wonders if even the smoke columns from the homes upon the cliff are praising "the one above"-responsible for his perceived beauty. This in one of many of his poems with a focus on the spiritual/ ethereal/ and wholeness in the universe.

-Gulls are still Everywhere   #1 visit-1972
The Long Hiatus Sept.-22-24-1986-# 7-   #6 visit 1976
The long hiatus made us return   Please
Bade us   See Old
    Book
Retire to the sea and be happy
Momentarily
Notice-one thing you can't see
Is a palm tree
So here are three from me
To thee.
O.K. ("Hello" in our guest book) Kerkoch-1985-9-24
                           Bend, Or

*with a melancholy
Tear or two
shed by Jean*

*To celebrate our prior
Pleasant memoires
Of Previous Stays-*   *Gud Valsigna*
*We popped the cork
Of a bottle or two-
And drank them
Toasting the good old*

Hi Lynn lift ['] em high.   *days. Pasted the label of one
on the opposite page [,] Hoping to
review it on other sunny days.
K-85*

There seem to be two separate poems here-The Long Hiatus and To Celebrate. In the first of the two, Dad draws palm trees and sea gulls above the trees at the left margin of the poem. As he mentions, palm trees are not found on this beach, but Mom and Dad also frequented the tropics, in particular, Hawaii. So maybe he missed them and wanted to interject one of their tropical getaways in with this Oregon coast stay. It seems that there had been a significant lapse in their travel to the Oregon coast for he writes about "the long hiatus" which made them return. For there they will find happiness even if only "momentarily". Dad also lists the dates of their first visit in 1972 and their sixth visit in 1976 to the right of the main body of the poem. He also suggests that the reader "See [the] Old Book" for these entries. His sentimentality seemed to lead him to categorize each and every visit they made and then revisit past stays upon the most recent. When he signs off at the end he says "Hello" to those who will read this entry.

In the second section of this two part entry-To Celebrate-Dad writes about all the memories that have accumulated since their first stay. So they popped a few corks to enjoy and toast "the good old/days". He even pasted one of the bottle labels (signed by them both) on the next page for future reference-hopefully on a future sunny day at their favorite place. The addition on the right margin is "Gud Valsigna" which I'm sure is a salutation in Slovenian. I don't know for sure what it means and not able to ask him anymore, but I'll take a guess-[To the good life]. On the left margin he writes "with a melancholy/Tear or two/shed by Jean"-to suggest she too is sentimental about their time here. Next, below this side-bar he says Hi to Lynn who he expects to read this salutation and suggests he make a toast in their absentia- "lift ['] em/high".

Note: There is some discrepancy about the dates included in these twin poems. The Long Hiatus is dated Sept.-22-24-1986, but at its end Dad writes Kerkoch [Americanized version of Krkoč] -1985-9-24, and then with To Celebrate he signs off K-85 too, but these poems are on the same page in the unit guest book journal, so maybe he just made a mistake. Which year he wrote these is impossible to determine. Also, these beach poems probably weren't all he wrote there over the years, for these particular ones from the Guest Books were some my then husband and I took photos of in just one of the units-The Penthouse-during one of our stays. Mom and Dad stayed in several different units, so I strongly suspect there are others not presented here but probably still in the beach place unit journals. At the end, Dad hoped to return one last time, and we kids made tentative plans to make that happen. But time, circumstances and their fragile states prevented it. I do hope they are still able to visit together often in some other form.

Epilogue

Mom had a clown collection. Dad knew she liked clowns and so he would buy her a piece from time to time. Some were quite expensive and exquisite. She displayed them in a cabinet with glass doors. I have the cabinet in my home and I've painted it with bright colors to compliment the colorful collection of clowns. I have thought about why she might have had such an attraction to clowns. As a child, I remember being frightened of them when I went to the circus where they were one of the attractions. Anyway, I came to believe that Mom had an affinity for them because clowns are mysterious. One can't see the person underneath all the paint and elaborate costuming. Mom was an enigma to me just as clowns are. I think Dad was the only person who came to understand her at all. Their relationship was intriguing to me. Maybe that is why I was so excited to find this album after their deaths. It helped me to understand them and their complicated relationship better. I hope Dad was right about their finding peace and comfort together in the forever after. I hope they have come to understand each other, to forgive, and to cherish. I hope they look down on us and bless us. I hope they have as much passion and fun as they did down here. I wonder if they have got to take that other cruise Dad dreamed of taking when, here on earth, the possibility had gone beyond them.

Original Poems

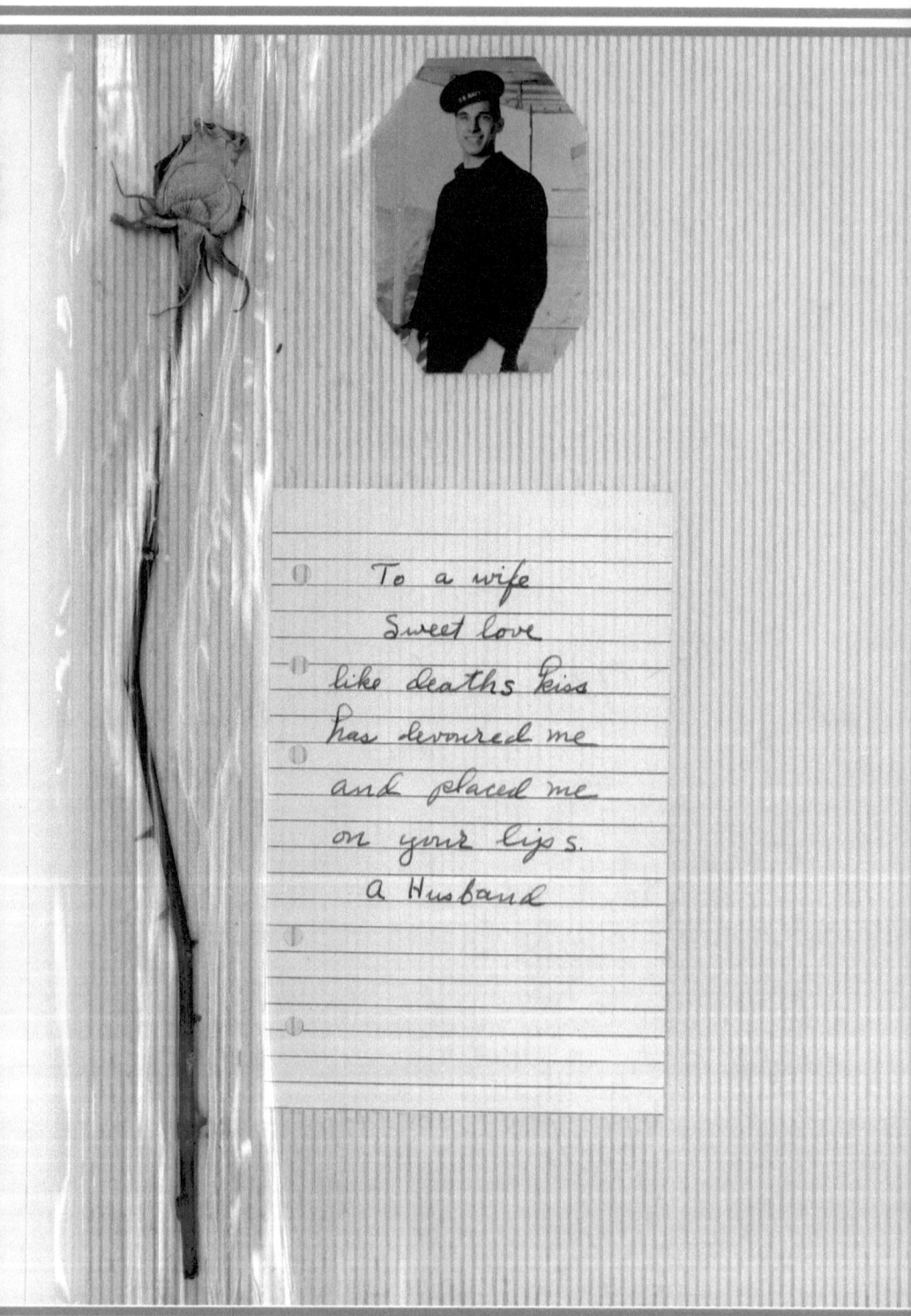

Its odd how can it be
the strange peace your presence brings me
In content I sit silently
my life passing pleasantly
Yes odd how can it be
Why should your presence do
    this to me
  as I sit silently.
Heart and mind alone won't tell
For time and time alone

#1

When alone it's easy to dream
and live in fantasy how
you will fight to save your
lover from impending tragedy,
  Yet in reality
more honest deeds requiring
greater bravery can be —
  to give your life to one
who only loves you in return
then recall the price men
  pay to pride and jealousy
and before you fall all acts of bravery.
True love lives in hearts of men
not tongues of Hipocrits who leave
  the battle to emotions
    as pride and jealousy
which soon devour the keepers
for he can never set them free.

#2
    Understanding is
  a simple deed
  a simple act
      ah!
    True love
      in fact.

#3   (corny)
  Hide from life
  It can be done
    But Death
  is never outrun.

2 lovers for the one I love may
reveal the way my heart feels.
But my love more like the
  seeds unseen — implanted
leads to untold multiplicity.
Then each in turn again —
  again to come with splendor
      to unfolding.
  Till the other like a taste
        of love
    Grows & Grows unending.

Dearest, when you are near
Countless times I've pondered,
"Why not reveal what lies
here beneath your breast"?
So it seems like Casano I
must pen my love or it
  will never be told,
and I wish you to know
my heart is never still
but forever expands
like the rush of a breeze
  through boughs of trees
Tenderly caressing and
  kissing the leaves.

Again - Again

The strings tug at my heart
and choke back all its efforts.

again again

That hollow feeling grips me
as we sit apart.

I feel your presence then would be
like -
 rain drops in the desert -
 a comet in the sky -

no -   more like

God, to one about to die.
This vision lies - then a
voice whispers -
Can this be - One
with flesh of dust

Touched -
with things that live eternally.

Dearest one only one
your sweetness and ways
remain a mystery to me.
As mine may seem to you.
Like the rose on the
vine your scent & sweetness
sublime transpose to me
a most important time

Hedonistic
Here Lies
No cares
No fears
No tears
No permanent alliance
No stone
No poem
Uncherished
Completely alone

Hearts heavy but my
chest feels void.
Can't understand it.
Stare, eyes moisten then dew.
Motionless the body weeps too.
Spirits gone a
thing of unquest
Found again only in rest.

Feel a patch of sunshine off to my left a bit
reach it?
Once thought I did.
Fed on its sweet substance was my everywhere.
Eyes open – Oh despair there is darkness everywhere

Here on earth at last
With others sharing a past
Escaped so well so long
Had a happy inner song.
Such a simple tune
now gone.

Today

today
  I thought of you alone getting dinner ready for our comming home
today
  On arrival not much was said but cherishment was our poem

  Then a peaceful meal later did portend
  How a regular evening was going to end
  In quiet love that does not shout
  But covers us like a warm mantle about

  For the laughter, cries, taunts and all
  are always of a spirit pleasurable to recall.
      Such simple things
          we d say
      God nothing better ever brings.

For Silence

The children are asleep
a fires crack is all I hear
On this night so deep and still.
I think about our quiet life
and wonder why beneath my
breast all thoughts lie dead.
Where is this match I seek.
I speak all day and much
at night but my dreams of
   you all lie unsaid.
Why so mute with tender phrases
- pure love - happiness - content - and more
when I feel the pleasure of there glow.
Could they if told lead to a fatal
   blow - no
But none will flow because of
of some tight unseen band

Embraced

I sat and half aloud tried long to compose
A short verse to tell you how I adore thee,
And though this feeling ran from my
heart along with the blood to permeate,
    a portion, to each part.

Dumfounded, as though we sat face to face,
no further words than these could this
pen trace other than to say; I truly live
   in adoration for you embraced.

                       Bob

JEAN - How I feel.   May 21, 1966

Like Bylon I must say I love you
with every pore. It sounds so sweet to me
like poetry the ever trite I love you.
I feel your presence next to me with drink
or sober always the same. Your soul &
body part of me our spirits together
as only we can know. A thought or
place in our hearts entwined
a common bond no other human can
share it's ours how pure how unique.
Our spirits know what I seek in the
words above — in depth of field —
In solitude you know what I feel for
we feel alike confident of love like
few alive. What a gift. What a life -
what a love. Cherish with ever increasing
feeling each year in its passing. Only
better because it was spent together
in bond of mutual love

I sit tonight with alcohol as an
an ally to set free a tongue so
tied when in front I can't say
what I feel so deep so fundamental
inside. Why not say over and
over again what in my heart
sits — Why not — When sober or
in regular course — I don't know
its never released. A few times
even with drink. I can't
explain this lack of voice
that pen allows & express
but not the voice. I feel
we play captive to our past
and though we try few
true feelings drive past our
artificial fringe to find

a place expressed
so if done even clumsily at
best my heart and
soul have been undressed.
To you my love I only feel my
heart and soul have been undressed.
I want you to know if you
said but a wish to me — If
I could grant it it would be.
I speak not of earthly wants
but of things I know are
more precious to you and
me. Like just a pat a
caress or more in jest or
for more serious cause. But
always with love and

and scope more broad than simple quest of emotion. For our settlement is greater than a brief emotional encounter for it lasts in spirit more than in flesh. So farewell tonight True love and may we see future union of soul and flesh as we have in past encounters — I hope your satisfaction lies with mine so all will be as well with you as it has been with me.

　　　　　To Love

It reads well with proper intent so feel you should get the ~~~~ feeling that I meant.

July 1967

Alone

Often if alone my thoughts drift
to you
Sweet pleasure often melancholy
binds me.

Alone silent joy feeds my spirit
and I pass an hour rich for that
one brief moment.

Threads

Threads of time together entwine
Each good moment adding another
the cord if death should part us
Unraveled through space
will still
join your heart and mine.

January 1, 1968

The simple things are best of all
Like a quiet day alone with you.
When only words of kindness pass
Like they very often do.

40. *April 6, 1968*

Long days
Long duties
More demand more
Deem more
Back - Brain Body
Beat
Retire - Refreshed
Repeat - Repeat - Repeat
yet.
Nearly Over

Drifts *February 19, 1968*

Un matters time or doing my mind
drifts — to you.
Encountering form and face.
Evenescent joy — passed.
Drifting doing.

Hate to see the baby cry
and you too —
I love you — I love you
What more can I do.

Tired

Much Toil
No help True
Children fuss
Till about two
On & On
Hours take a tole
Wearyness hits
Yet more to go
Holidays too few
then
Turmoiled years
are through
Only love left
Will it do.

September
1962

Had a coctail
thought of you.
During Dining
you drifted
through
Listened to
a lecture
interspersed
by you.

Keep drifting
back ~~through~~
Nothing else
I want to do.
you ~~can~~ made
me happy
through &
through

September, 1967

We drift together
Separate shells
Touching at will
  and random
Time passed paths
parallel - converge
then merged
continue onward.
Blessed with
  purpose and need.

January 14, 1971

Dreams
Exist - Drift
about - float
freely - Flit
through - mostly
of you.
Moments of
pleasure. Instant
warmth - with
residual glow -
don't want to
let it go -
Ephemeral -
concept grows

October, 1970

Fasten for a moment your
  eyes to mine.
Dream of golden grapes
ripened on a vine.
Oh fastening sweeter
than their wine.
Draws back - silent bliss
  sublime.

2-16-71

thanks —

It is as warm as your line but not nearly as beautiful

———

Sorry about the salad the tender care was obvious.

Alone reflecting
what would I say
if we were alone
some day,
no intruders
just ourselves
on a short
grand holiday
Would we just
pass the time
of day
nothing's not
what we would say

No but talk of
dew flowers,
love and of
running barefoot
too
And again I'd
declare my
love to
you.

Reflecting Ryan's
9-15-72
& Kissah
1:30

Mental Imagry

Sit and philosophically examine
the world at present and in rest.
Reflect on now and on the past.
Where do pleasures lie
      mainly un mental,
   sadly in physical repast.
So thank you now because my
mental pleasure is aglow.
Contrasted to less than one man per
millenium touching aphysical sublimily
a state so familiar to me
my dreams are ten times ten than
     a touch and
the aftermath times ten again.
And yet the state of our affair
Lies at one for me on a scale of
   Ten relative to infinity.

Kerr 72

Erased

Ran north along the ocean for a mile or so
Found a lonely segment of beach
Houses high no ladders led below
There alone before an incomming tide
I traced a message dedicated to
the birthday of my love.
      Perchance
it happened to be slightly late
Mind dwells on the message none will see
Except those departed and me
Like a mind etched from birth to rest
the incomming tide will soon erase
      every trace
before she passes that perfect place.

                        JRK
                        7-14-73

Yet Alive

Complicated thing you make my
heart sing
Yet your cut subtle nuance drops
my affect to nothing.
Un perfect as I am — I am
my bag good or sad.
hear so now
The trend is set - set hard
natural thing. Un natural way
Exposed to heat will
steel's temper hold
Or will
the sear effect collapse
leaving alone a deserted
lifetime of my own.
Sadly will I say
I died tomorrow - today.

Heppity   K - 11-73

Dust?

Stardust formed cosmos
born of your special
   sellar dust.
In celestial reaction
has captured my form
and vast as it may be
the remaining nebulae
mean much less
   to me

K

Intangable love - not so
in after glow - can have
a melancholy sad
Mellowed thing
Permits a being
Alone reflected in each
breath nurtured
by sight and touching
need.

K 13

Its grown to be that the only
important things happen occasionally
Don't know what I've done for
you but I know what you have
done for me and as

Brandy flowers good wine an you
all belong on the same line.
No matter where I go they are
synonamous with a good life flow.

On Loving

A little at a time you have come to dominate my heart and mind.
Your constant sight has been the seed.
Consumated thing don't understand your power
your haunting refraine insane.

What shall I say or show that I care to expose heart and minds affairs.
Words a light touch.
  perhaps best that eye shine telegraphs the message from my mind.
May I possibly than choose all three as a gift from me
If by a quirk of fate am not alone when touched so Tenderly by fate.

K-73

Fantastectasy

Watch T-V's idealistic caress.
Gentle kiss eyes burn with idolitry.
Suddenly your motions like a
symphony rush to my memory.
Followed by a wish - a single
light kiss to transfer imagry to
Tender reality.
Then a slow light brush of
your cheek or mouth emoting
effectively
A nod hand squeeze part and
emerge to fantastectasy.

K. 73

Just Because
you are part of me
Heart and soul of me
absence felt
immediately
Come back
resume your piece
of me.
K. 3-18-74

Coast Collection

Grease is of little concern
Solidifies in any urn and
scoops out great so why bellyache
Peace here is the deal of appeal
to nit pick about grease is unreal
Was fun to pen this rebuttal
Because the view is the whole bubble
Each has a rainbow you know

Gulls ever glide past
Constantly searching the sea
    serenity
Waves constantly hush ashore
Green white gray
    possibly forevermore
Unique combination seen but once
by few purchased ashore
near Overlook view
    joy ensue bursting to
    Tranquility
fleeting seldom virtue
    found
Here where its presence surrounds.

10.74

Dust

Stardust formed cosmos born
Your special stellar dust
In celestial reaction has
captured my form and vast
as they may be the remaining
nebulae mean much less
      to me

          K-74

Flaws

What is this lack in me
Will time let me see
Or shall I keep my blindness
    to reality.
Taking it to eternity
Should I lessen my ways
    allow insight
to rip away this blight
Make ammends
See the light
Doing what is generously right
Allowing all in loves sight
    to live demand free
      happily
In true equality
Will it ever truly be.

          K 11-74

In Spring

Will we be there again
that high place.
Sun and view bottles of wine
we two – dream and joyfully
chatter of winter gone
summer yet to be.
How long will fortune stay
repeat – repeat again – again
and still once more.
Then possibly above at timeless
equal intervals knowing no more
joy than we share now when
our eyes meet in some
selected retreat
to share at once an entire
entwined past.
No other way exists more
perfectly for two.

K. H

Review

Twenty five years spent by two
Now in melancholy review
Spin planet on time
I remain sublime of mind
Content in the past
Knowing the future can't promise
or possibly hold the
pleasures the past has allowed to unfold
Where will the next twenty five lead
Don't really care
Have had my share
But
there may still be
further revealing of minds
Wine · picnics · dinners with you
Christmas, Easters and masses for two
A toast
Oh · future allow
the children to see
the fate time held for me

K-75

Modern Flight

Hey awake at night
with everslight uptight
While dual fancies bite
then build a bridge
with either
hand to the right
Closeness —
So blight
Caresses make it bright
Wishes
Fulfilled tonight

K-6-75

To You

Love
to long
to little
said
to late
of that which
dealt us kind fate
I
thank
you now
for the ulti-
mate.

K-75

Flower

Youthful bloom
offered accepted
& negated over
the years
Tender flower
Petals taken
softly
in hand.
Her heart
carried
with
tender intent
intact
held close
one score
near ten
more

K 75

Come Alive

Six thirty five – Come alive
Breakfast for four later more
Add dishes to those behind the door
Hustle out water and run
The fridge to empty no fun
Lug fruit, vegetables meat and more
Clean em all. Clean em all
It's later. lunch for the bunch
and an extra few – Out again
Bills, prancing, gymnastics too
Run around Run around its almost two
Hustle – Hustle – water and dinner anew
    Out and in – in and out
Phone – Phone answer it please
Will there be coctails for duo
Quiet – Peace – maybe a moment
Dinner – Dishes – Garbage and more
Bath – Noise – Slam – Bark and Clang
    In an out – Out an in.
Workers come – Workers go
Can't sleep – Weary dreary
    Toss muscles ache
Six thirty five – Come alive.

            K-75

Friendly Skies

Many times
These skies were
coursed in unity
Was burgandy with company.
Today in solitarity
        it
passed in routine pleasantry
none of
The usual revelry
No cementing verbal ties
nudge or caress
only drawing round each eye
    as
Thoughts trace old ties of
crosses through azure skies
so cheers
may our next trips be
anyone you take with me.

K.
5-7-57

If not with you I
order
martini twist & olive
too.
what would you
do. K-76

Service Compris
Our dinner price
includes service.

Figment.

Scheduled mini-airliner manditory early arrival
Quiet time
Three hours four beers two papers later
The urinal was my grand theater
Then the lobby till quarter of nine
Retreat to the restaurant—just in Time
Ideal corner booth for two
Prime
Prawns a Tenth of wine
Reflected
That just passed
was easy to see
that
During that interval
none seemed to posess
Or act likes we two
Then I knew
the corner booth
really held two
me and
the figment of you
Ten
The airliner is due.

K-75

Rings

Watching movies solitare
Softly drifting rings
that break
Graceful floating
fleeting forms
Silently
Drift more
Your countance
saw it appear
Drifting memories
by
Beautiful things
just
like Rings.

K- 2-76

Life

Quiet reigns
Smoke rings emerge
Gradually enlarge
as they move
ever more slowly away
Perfect symetry slipping
Gently developing
more beauty and form
stratify then drift
to blend imperceptably
Each
in its unique way
Unseen currents direct
their fate
Silently
we are born
Thanks.

K. 4-76

VERY FINE LIQUEUR COGNAC BRANDY
On 4-13-76
what more could I do to share my great respect for you
J & F Martell
COGNAC
CORDON ARGENT
4/5 QUART   Martell & Co   80 PROOF
COGNAC - FRANCE
PRODUCE OF FRANCE
for your delight
at your prof.
PRODUCED AND BOTTLED IN COGNAC (FRANCE)
SOLE DISTRIBUTORS FOR THE U.S.A.
THE JOS. GARNEAU CO.
NEW YORK, N.Y.

My prayer.   Please   for you

Let time pass
To
wipe all sadness from your eyes
Time
bless with peace
set her mind at ease
Rest contented
new mind with inner bliss
Time
then Transfered to
bodily serinity
Lord so may it be

K. 76

Airport Story

See the couples at the port
Watch them - Silent sit drink and stare - Now
a Newv-engrossed pair window seat abreast
 Oh. Joy. - Wait.
His hair is gray her skin is white and fair
 No bands lie there no lasting
  bond
 Its born to be short and physical I fear.

Another couple of similar vein - Bearded beau
and clinging packsack girl converse abreast
 against the wall
  Alas bandless all his composure cool
 uncommitment here I fear.
More starers - some young some old filter
 in and out - an endless stream.
Unless 2 couples or more share the surrounding air
see little action there. But always nothing
from those not against the wall
  Were do we sit in the promincle
Against the wall - laughing close bands and all.

K- 12·76
P.I.A.

SEE

Need me —

Spirit call me now —
Out of that deep financial
solitary ravine.
Where I have been.
Need me down in your hole
Could I be
your magnetic pole —
the North. South all your soul
Need me alone — a day — two or three
My direction I pledge will be
 magnetic true
Directly to you

K. 12-20-76

3-29-75
And more

Eat drink read the news
View the ocean chase the blues
Sip more Beer records soar
above the oceans incessant roar
Swim and run for exercise
Floated Beautiful Kites in
    azure skies
Depart and start to reminisce
About a return to all this

Lined up a place to eat
Both Half Shell. Sounded neat.
  But the din – did me in
  Before I ordered my first round.
  Retreat the Ambassador
  as I walked by seemed neat.
  Peace, Palm room one
  look around nostalgia
  abound — Was a place for us
  a cocktail or two – before
  a dinner you see.
  The view at 82 was of
  palms inside and out

Nearness

Think and dream
  of you
  intermittantly
The whole day through
  Did you know
  the only amiss is
  simple nearness
Close to you don't need
  verbal exchanges
Silence and proximity
  alone produce
  sublimity
    Thanks

K-4-77

Should tell you daily
love you
Easy thing to do
But routinized
Drift along unverbalized
Tragedy
Sudden shift
to late so great
is deaths rift.

K-77

2-7-77 — 9:00 PM
  Tide Out
Alone then three descend
 one hundred steps to
night time quiet beach
above Two stars shine through
 then whisps of
 air suspended dew
A long arc, lights up on
 the hills
 Both filter through
  Trees and dew

50° No wind at all
Oceans white cresting waves
 move
Four five at a time even smaller
 toward shore
 while
 ~~lights~~ up on the hill
Smoke columns move
 straight up
Are they fingers of praise
 to one above.
            KW

Thank You

Thank you for being there
Thank you for the way you care
Thank you for what we share
Like the weekends at the beach
Coffee wine and coctail time
Quiet talks about the kids
in those active luncheon pits
Thank you for being here sweet one
    I hold so dear
      Thank you.

          K.
          10.77

Sides

Refused
a partnership lawyer post meeting dinner invitation
  Traveled -
home in tired hasty anticipation
  . Did
I - We misenterpert the intonation of my
mates initial incantation.
  To
reply with rapid irrational irritation
  Bilaterally
destroying the expected exhilaration.
  Hurt
both toss attempting a restless sleep
  Dawn are
there minute possibly asymetrical repairs
  Drawing
on past strength to the rent progressively resolving
  Never
to completely fill again oh. Tiny scar
  Toast
past happy times - future hold more of the primes $K_8 \pi$

Why

Partially watch the craps on T.V.
Light a Partagas and meditate
Wonder did I help you down
Think as I scan a financial sheet
How can I help. What can I do
Change my fibre. Reshape the past
      Possibly the former
    Certainly not the last
Past seamed right to me
      but
did it help Trigger your insecurity
Now what will the future bring
   The good or bad for three.
We see no pleasure unless you are free
      So
Cast the devil out to sea and
resume your usual Tranquillity.
      Because
we are still entwined Nora you and me
      in
   mutual dependency.

                    K.
                    5.78

Dear Heart.
Love you in my quiet way
When you near its the best
    of my day
Even though I may not have
    the sense to say
Daily I feel closer to you
    in every way.
Thats why I become sad
of heart even when
others part.
  Remain   K-78-6-6
my dear heart.

        When
How about a holiday
    for two
With walks and talks
    hopefully
    in the sun
Some shopping for
    nick nacks
Leisurely noon time snacks
Breakfast at pool or
    oceanside
Rent a cycle go for a ride
the tempo will be slow
    Say the word
    and we will go.
              Love
               Bob
                9-78

        Love you
As you are tonight asleep
    Tired and distraught
    Reposed at needed rest
before our usual daily Tests
        Routine
    Does me down
at illness pleasure or at sin
acts that really never meet
    mostly ends incomplete
Goodness scores in heart we know
So hail our status quo
Oh to prognisticatPons to
        the better
          To
        greater days
    than those ago
A toast to pleasures
            that
count our past delights
        Oh arise
A fresh miracle at noon
reborn new complete
    fresh two.
            K-11-2-78 x10

Up Again

Makes me sad to see you down
   Lacking your usual smile when
      I come around
     Bottom aching
   Appetite not up to par
Turning down our usual lunches
     in bunches
Different we two as night and day
   But not in pride I must say.
   Oh see our partnership
Don't depreciate your game
   You are full of the stuff
  Ladies and queens are made of
So I toast you my love
Like the Chinese on the boats
The lines and cards today
     say
   Better eighties are on the way
So soon in a southern clime
    God willing
We will have a close wonderful time
    It says so in
    your palm line.

                 Kirk.
                 1-79

1-27-81 Guess who I am
          or where.
          Can you read
          it Dear.   single penning
                        no rewrite or
                        correction to
Was an interesting day because   this
I got to stay. at the hospital   recollection.
for a prolonged delay.   K.
It was only an inconvenience for me
Because all I had to do was stay. ↔ Check the
Drive to Burns was fun and games.   newspaper
an M.D. in Fog on snow and slush   for the
with a tired driver perusing the Pmt. events of
Time was not so swift esp. after the the day.
snow plow drifts. at less than 35 m.p.h. One Dead
In Burns in good shape know Republic 2 on the
will not make the trip but ready to go way.
if the flo is 50 50.   Auto acc.
Transition is great - here ready to eat. up Butchers
Ponderosa is the choice - ½ liter of wine way.
Believe it or not Chicken proves to be Prom.
the pick of mine — and I eat every course citizen
thinking back in time - Its been 12 whs. you
since you and I were here life of mine. had
Salut to a fine time and hope a   a
replay of same will be mine. ℱ Love K. 1-27-81. hard
                                        day
                                        today.
                                        K.

Pine Room

Solemn bored faces in the countryside
Hear names like Curley and Stud
Bulky guys & big boots and hats
Waitresses aged and homely but
fast on their feet
Believe it or not a gray haired
lady passed gas on her way to the door
They file in at a steady pace.
Stays in general are quiet & short
whats happened that 30 yr. old
couple silently eating not sharing
empty stares
Look around you will see it all
Pine room drama ceiling to floor.

a pen

A fine simple point
A collection of ink above
Transferred by mind and hand
To an adoring you for the
 one I love in
  script
That can be large or small
To convey miraculously
Any feeling mind to mind
A period of tenderness
recorded for all time
To write with such a pen
 is extacy for
It writes I love you so
 delicately.

 K.
 4-81

5-5-82

BURNS #2 But can you read it.

I ordered a full course
for myself. but found it
is enough for two or at least 1½.
Ordered the T-Bone not
Chicken cuz you weren't there.
Didn't notice had the small.
But I must say - Big is
 the way.
→ Found there was no big anyway.
Then I have only one hint.

"Cut next to the bone &
work your way out on
the N.Y. side. Leave the
rest for the dogs outside.
Made it early. Done by
7:30. - Crowd not as
~~burly~~ sturdy. - waitress
still burly.

Looked over my shoulder
was not sure but lo &
behold he didn't appear

Sweet Trip

Back in Time
Old movie sent via waves
Hawaii local. Fifties scene
Purity patriotism and J. Wayne
but only
Small background fragments
jarred my memory and
I swam into a
nostalgic extacy.
My mind engaged in
Fleeting moments of sublime
pleasure.
Had you been there
those floating sweet Laylonnie
strains shared in silence would
have been sweeter at the time.
But sharing with a written page
also has its place I feel.

Love
K
12·19·83

Feb. 83

Sitting in Burns you see
watching the crowd.
In a new Outpost
Pine room was closed.
Chicken was greasy
But only 9.95 2 salads wide
Plate was cold.
Butter was Oleo and
the service was slow.
Guess what I did read
the paper
also
thought of L.A. č Sweetye
then – Don't know why
skipped to Bud McCusker
He still works you see
Hoblingly
They mention White but
never Bud. So Sad.
I hope when we go
Someone. Anyone will say.
Eather of the K's are going aw[ay]

March 30, 83   *unpublished*
Sat in the Pine Room
  without you
  thought to myself —
Thirty plus years of quest
    Gave
An arrowhead collection
    To two
Equal in some odd way as
  I see Thee and me
So with deep respect and
  a degree of awe.
I will buy if I can
This symbolic memento
  of the life they knew.
  and dedicate it to you
So we can reflect
  with due respect
What will be left
    of us
Oh museum poor lost idea
Now you are to be
  a symbolic memento.
      may be later K-83

SWEET Thing
Down tonight. Hope the A.M. is Bright.
Rockefeller Square - Lots of flowers there.
One Bless God Bless stay fresh.
Tonight. Sampled the street and
things to eat.
But no big discovery my sweet.
One place I hit. Toodori
oven. Tried for the Bread
But don't know yet. Will
I get the dough. But I
will let you know.
Remember one thing you never
spoil anything only make it
supreme or if not well a little less
    so.   K. 10.17.83

Jean
In a moment of tender time
Our fingers may entwine
Form a knot of love
Eyes shine be mine
Gentle squeeze a
Cheek kiss - Brush
a Tress of hair
Its all There
Love
    Bob
    84

Harry's Bar   7:00 p.m.
I sat alone shed a tear
  you were not there.
Am alone 14% too much
    alone.
Crowd not quite the same
    Like us
    a parody
    Bee
I asked why - Oh see
  No theater
  oh me
I suspect. May I
may we be an
  oddity.
  No. May we
Last night was
 "Sh—" you see
Love thee.

BRandy in the Plaza Bar & Cigar then to bed by car.
7:30.
Set it up "Alexander & Craig" — manitaller for 2.
Table 11 or. Sed 7 cocktails then Dinner at 8:00.
Lovely K
Harry's
  1:55

Jean
Bar's a lonely place
 Solitude
Cigar fills the space

Smoke spirals into the air
Carries a dream
Oh smoke ring
ethereal thing
 you Bring
Backs the memory of
a prior place
Sweet thing you
Hold an everlasting place
 no more space. K·8·23·85

I love Jean she makes
me go out of my bean as you
have seen. Cheer up the
chicken soup is good for body
and soul. and it will be blessed (Job 6?)

Paper and Me
Hour 2:45
Missed you no Steak
Where were you tonight
Had a nice flight.
 Shrimp
Brown Bread and
 Bean Soup
Oh Fried chicken
Tomorrow I'll poop
Ice creame and
 coffee –
 Finee –
 Oh Gee
No cigar you see
Love Thee K·
 8·20·85
 you are
 part of my life
 Long
 heart.
 Tonight.

Day By Day

Mind chronicles your faraway stay
Still feel I love your every way
Wondering what we will first say
On the comming November Sunday
    Not much but
My mind and heart will glow that day
Then after you recover from the lag
  To toast after the long delay
  with a chosen burgandy Romanée
On possibly as you wish
the one fourteen will be the dish
Than hopefully Together we shall lay
  In heavenly foreplay.
    I pray
  Day By Day
      K
    11-15-85

7-16-94

Dearest Jean:

I now know the month will be m[uch] harder for you than me. But the deg[ree] was a complete surprise to me. It must be because the children are no longer home since when we were yo[ung] during the course of a year we spent less time together than we do now. Probably 2-3x more/yr. Even with all my recent and present separations. My 2 calls on the 15th probably hur[t] more than they helped. I will try

write cards while I am in Europe as often as possible. It is not a war I am not in the service and the time will go more quickly than you imagine.

Hope you can read my small writing.

Our Bond is firm and good. We are lucky but please take some joy in my trips like I take joy from your visits with Norbert.

With Sweet Sorrow
Love, Bobby

Flames

Like fires warmth and beauty
   you still fill my eyes
      Reflect.
Starts with much ado a flicker
   with some smoke then
      slowly
Bursting into rising flames
     That
  spread at an ever increasing
     pace
     Then
  Slowly by embers to be replaced.
Transformed to an orange red sea
   then to slowly fade away
    Like silent aging
Expirenced the fuss smoke and ado.
Have felt the motion the flame
   the flow of love
     and now
like the embers inside I still
     glow.

            K. 12-21-85
         1st Day of Winter

```
                     LDA015(1047)(1-006625A246)PD 09/03/85 1048
ICS IPMPTUF PTL
02521 09-03 0843A PDT PTUE
ICS IPMLD04
4-010673S246 09/03/85  A015-1047
ICS IPMBNGZ CSP
  5033820179 TDBN BEND OR 2 09-03 1025A EST
PMS FRANK KERKOCH RPT DLY MGM, DLR
CENTURY PLAZA HOTEL
AVENUE OF THE STARS
LOS ANGELES CA
LOVE YOU.
    JEAN
    1314 NORTHEAST 9 ST
    BEND OR 97701

01-SF (R5-69)  1035
```

I reply
Implicitly
Simplicity is best
To express
The minds sublime
If done on Time
Here are
Franks
Thanks
L. you 2
9.5.85

See love stories on T-V
Read Shakespere Holmes Whitman and
        Thoreaux
Feel the essence of Romeo & Juliet etc.
Vicarious projections abound but none
    are any more profound than
        those I have found

Stupidity

More than two hours late
For our anticipated date
Nicest thing I can emulate
Our meeting at the estate
  What should I do
When my eyes percieve you
  I old fool
Outward expression dull
  Emotion null
Inside not TRUE
The sight of you
That simple view
  Content
With internal chaos
  Transpires
  So
Stupidly take refuge in the mind
  Such assininity
Forgive the complacency
With its utter stupidity
Love isn't absent minded
  enmity or at
least it should not be ✗ 6-5-86

(TURBULANCE)

wish for Jean.
Oh Morpheus sweet
spirit what secret
calls do you answer
Reveal your ways.
To peaceful rest I pray
Calm spirit fill my nights
  & Rest
Let loose my Tensions
of the mind
Relax my muscles in
short time —
Wake me rested & sure.
To face the day so sure

In Less than a Day

Motored over the pass
through snow up to my
Arrived wind howling
and some downpour
Rain hail - felt pale. Then
Nestled in after
fish and chips
Lolled away the rest
  of the day
Evening walk. Small talk
Dinner at pier 101
Watching it snow
Then like magic
Wouldn't you know
Winds cease to blow
Clouds go
And in the cool still night
The stars shown bright
  Some night.

Jean -
I love you.
Your form
Your grace
Your ever
lovely face.
The extacy of
your embrace
Indellably
in place
my total being.
To embrace

K - 9-21-87 2:00 AM. Redo. with 7 roses.
Always thinking of you. Tour 25

Wish

You felt better
more of the time.
Might that you would
become more sublime.
Scars of the past
Oh dissapear.

Sadness of the past
is best left behind.
Consentrate only on
the best of Times.
Since you posess more
beauty of body and mind
Than almost other
live womenkind.   Kuk. 9-15-87

Thanks
For
Being you plus all you do.
Being kind your natural state of mind
Being forebearing & understanding.
Being there for every family care
Seeing to each daily need.
  and every feed.
In tender silence you fill my every
    need.
        Keiki love
         1.25.87

I don't want to talk about
            it.

Senior citizens need lots of love too.

An Answer

How beautiful life is from
the outside looking in.
Simplicities uncomplicated
niceties in panoramic view.
Quiet times of harmony espied.
   Aspen leaf in a breeze
    Peace of mind
From the outside looking in
   is easy to find momentarily
But to hold for a prolonged
period thats the question
And the answer is death.

               Kirk
              4-25-88

Mind Set to Rose

Mind program set in youth
Unconsciously incendentally.
Fused inperceptably.
Non consequential Trivia
        magnified.
Color the future improperly
    into a gray black hue
        Analyze
the works match them to the
        offending deeds.
        See
The folly of the guilt.
    Rehue color anew
Imbued a new Tint the Rose is you.

            Ksh. 5-1-88

See you tonight God willing

Soft You Are

Soft of heart of touch
Love you so much
Tender in your mind
With a heart so so fine
And - You partly mine
Oh life can be so devine
  The verse is short
       and small
My love for you to me is all
  That I can give
So long as I will live.

                    Friday
                Kirk 5-13-88

Can you read my script.
       tonight.

Erased

Ran the Ocean – Wasn't any message left in the snow
Sand prints all wiped clean
Realized them all
Erased like evenescent dreams
Imperfect solitude your spell descends
While alone without a friend
Stare
Empty space
Surf pounding at every visible place
Solitude erased
Melancholy replaced
by steady beats as each perfect wave thrusts
then repeats
Slowly the sand shift to end the empty blend
Bliss reimbraced
Satisfied reality returned
Embraced daydreams replaced with ages aches and
pains even in this blissful place
then
perfect pounding symphony dispells all – and ends.

With Jean

Quiet time of life we are in
Less fuss than in our youth has been
Peaceful naps for me easily begin
After a casual luncheon
Off to bed – nestle down
To restlessly toss around
Till bird songs at dawn
Call us from bed to bound
Still wonderful to see you around
With the love we have found
Let it last as it has in the past.

Dec. 11

F.R.K.

Jean The

Rose in the family without a thorn
Why starry eyes were you born
It's on the wall for everyone to see
The four belonging to you and me
Chiseled set the entire clan
Satisfaction predestined since it began
Having earned happiness and peace
Hope the future grants you these.
Were I God I would heed all your pleas
Those you request while on your knees

By: Bobby
1-8-89
for Jeanie

Ocean Scene
View was supreme
As you Jean lovely thing
Were you could not have been
Doty not supreme
Beringer Beaujolais 87
F./Th. with food was heaven
Bowl of tiny stoxan ricking
Good almost as your
 succulent being
But tho best on the menu
For you was not of venue
Since for you poached salmon
is not but a lemon
think of you when youre not here
Don't die before me dear K'g's

I See Not — So Hot

Sorry when
   I fortuitously make you sad
Happy when
   Such makes you glad.
When you ail
My psyche goes pale.
Unable to help
   I despair.
Your spirit
   in disarray
Forty down
   about twenty to go.
Let's try
   to make the best
Of the
   rest of the show
Might I
   change myself.
Open the door
And let
   your heart talk more
Of the
   complex being
Hard for
   my seeing.
Things far
   ago in the past
Great differences cast
But one
   fact endures
Body and soul
   I really am yours.

Need your glasses for this one

R.E. Morses per name for D.P.K. today
6-7-89

Frances a Lass
Without an I in her name.
We who know you understand same.
Face angelicly framing deep lovely eyes
Racing mind tending others with more than sighs
Around always aiding all family members in need.
Never shirking duties to products of her seed.
Caring year after year happily chronically tired.
Endlessly spending life mind love inspired
Sleep in peace to end only in heaven retired.

With love— K 2-16-90

Life Sentence

Who is to blame?   Lets play a game.
At one messy pants
Naughty girl
At Two a single error
        Bad thing
At three her they did not see
At four who permanently closed the door
At five one Time she childless died
At six no use again just never tried
At seven as always she would blindly mind
At eight her loyalty did not really matter.
By nine constantly sadder.
By ten confusion was the norm.
By eleven she guessed she did not belong
By twelve her heart held only a sad song
By thirteen guilt permanently set
By fourteen very little heart left
By fifteen body and spirit bent.
Seeping slowly with the years
The last of hope drops with the tears.
Wonder if there is one to caress
Does it end as such for this sweet lass.
To long for permanent release
From a verdict wrongly pressed
Upon a guiltless one that was oppressed
How sad is there no reprieve
From such inanimality but death
Or cleanse yourself with my tears please

Kzik
09·788·90

Demise

Belly's bloated was blurted out
Tender hand depart
Elated voice drops low
Disappointments flow
Alas no martini glow
Error unretrievable
In an unbelievable stew
Mistake - love you
Know such moments
are regretable few
Thats one I blew

Love Kirk 10·28·90

My Heart

Back in forty one
Saw a perky bit of sun
Rose again in forty six
Heart played tricks
    Mind too
     Then
Knew then what to do
   Marry you
Close now is sunset time
   Retrospect sublime
For heart and mind
It could be an eternal find
  Late Valentine   Bob 2-18-91

Difference

Hard to understand.
Harder to learn.
Each marching to
Ones own band.
Our fires others burn
Escaping the lighters hand
Others ways are hard to
  grasp.
Like hand fuls of dry
  sand.
In time one hopes to be
At least a player in
  the other's band.
But if love is a partner
  in the batter
  (over)

Happy Birthday You
you know I will think of
  you.
Many Times each day of
  you.
walking, running, working
  of you
and with coctails Too
  of you —
then a Tear or two
  appear for you.
  (OVER)
Bobby 7-18-91

To Thee

Beautiful Wife
Delight of my life
Shy Butterfly
Glint in my eye
Happy hello
Heart a-glow
Of love. I know
Gift from above
Short simple poem
To one I love
Happy 63rd 7-18-91 Bobby

Yourself
To Jean   with Tears

Your eyes don't see
Your ears don't hear
  But inside
Inner feelings of fear
That are not clear
Perceptions erroneously
  Imprinted
  Personality
In youth traumatically
Ah: Outside EYES see
  Outside ears hear
And with gut reality
  embrace
the true inner grace
  Yourself. Bobby 9-20-91

Near You

Want to be near you
My mind near you
Body too near you
Feel the memories of you
Mind pictures appear
when we are apart
Feel content when we
eat, sit, sleep and
Travel with leasure
meals and tours,
wine coctails even
Beer are better with you
Hope there is an after
world for us too
All this and more
near you

Kah - 10-28-94

To Me

Super fine lady so demure
Damsel sweet and pure
Giving more
Taking less
Embodyment of unshelfishness
Of mind and body in beauty
Born.
With pain and undeserved
Torment born.
May the future yet portend
A fate of better end
Deny all faltless guilt
Becoming restless free
To see yourself as
you appear.
To me.

Bobby S - (10-11) 94

Signs of Love

Feel and see them every day.
Things that you best say.
Reflected in as I go on my way.
Towels clothes for us to wear
    at work or play.
Coffee breakfast lunches snacks
    and more
Thought Touches seen everywhere
Floors swept carpet care dishes
    to prepare.
Apples salads the best to eat
Tenderly chosen one at a time
with all of us in mind.
Done if sick or well
Self sacrifice and prayers for us
Smiles and hugs so fine
Done with eyes that shine
Graceful beauty kind
    loyal and TRUE
Beautiful through and through
    Jean That's you 12-7-95

    Bob
    & Happy
      Tom

Maybe

She and me
Married we be
Me and she
To the other
Others to me
Eyes for none but thee
Oh Queen Bee
Only you I see
See you only me
Maybe a score
Left possibly more
Be I with one I adore
No more.

Bobby
1-8-95

To Jean

Dove

Helped me up when I was
nothing.
Never let me down
Kind dove cooing each time
I came around.
Laughed and cried together
With children we are bound
Decade after decade to become
More tightly wound
Passing toward eternity
Some peace we have
Found.

& Love and Trust
Bob Feb. 9th 1995

Wishing Well

Love to see you happy
Hate to see you sad
Your body is still firm
With shoulders so square
Back upright and not round
Still solid to caress.
Appitite is usually dandy
Coctail partner super handy
Thoughtful generous and kind
Oh! Woman super fine
Delivers love sublime
I will be forever thyne
If my wish upon a star
Please miracle cure appear
For the one I hold so dear
So I would never need
 another tear
And pain never more to feel.
So carefree we would be
 Me and Thee.
 Dis-comfort free
  Bobby 5-16-95

QUEEN ELIZABETH 2

See

We eat together
Both grow older
And less bold
 Nevertheless
Are most in bliss
When we are not amiss
But in mutual bliss
Like Sunday A.Ms
At breakfast time

Cheers or Ciao
Zivjo two.
Bobby Love
You

31-96

CUNARD

A Day

Sunny A.M. on Baptism Day
As Todd an Liz spends
a morning at play.
Breakfast served in a leasurely way.
Todd & Doug go out to play
While Joan puts dishes away
Every one scrubbed then in
finary dressed
Out to the chapel we Trek

As all the others are met.

Ceremony follows as the prayer
Words the principles say.
With water cleaning all sins away
Peacefully recongrate in 9th St.
Before we all meet again to eat

over
please

Queen Elizabeth 2

Remember?

I Remember how when were more carefree
Your eyes would shine when you looked at me
And mine, I am sure, would shine back to thee
Recalling too how beautiful you seemed to be
Your form so perfect your face pristine
In elderly years, altered by time
Your beauty of body, mind and soul
Remain unbelivably fine
Still flawless in my mind totaly sublime
Approaching the end of the line recall our time
I hope with some peace and pleasure in mind.

Bucky. 8-27-97

P.S. Maybe we could replay just one time.
On the Queen Elizabeth line in the sumatime.
Or maybe drop a dime on the S.S.T. line.

CUNARD
Queen Elizabeth 2
1995 Golden Route World Cruise

Forlorn.

Who what was this man so tall and stately.
Now bent, thin, frail, gray yet quiet grandly.
Time brings this heritage innately.
Hands now thin wan Tremble sadly.
At mass he stands bowed now humbly
Praying waiting for a death that's timely
 Nothing more reverently sublimely.

Sweet Sorrow Mon Amie

Part each A.M. go around
At times things get me down
No longer as carefree boy.
Treating worries like a toy.
Problems now are everywhere
Shaking them off is not simple fare
Ah! but soon we won't be there
I know that you must see
How sweetly I think of thee
Together we seem to be mainly
In each others proxsimity
If I am gone your form
From my mind is never gone.
Actually here with you I
would rather be.
Thats why the plans I make
Usually we together take.
So new conversations,
We may more easily plato
Without you Trips for me
are hard to make.
Because my heart I must
partially forsake

Pardon my darker moods
My Trips to outer space
I am not perfect you see
So my love for you is
not free
It comes with a penalty
The penalty is me

~~Bobby~~
95 - to 4-8-96

The Waterfront Hilton Beach Resort

Love you Jean
Yes I do
Composing as I sit
in my own Pew
your the best
Better than the rest.
The things you do
are good all though
So you see I love you

Bobby
11-23-97

The above is only for your eyes

21100 Pacific Coast Highway, Huntington Beach, CA 92648
Telephone 714-960-7873
Reservations 1-800-HILTONS

The Management Group inc.

Etherial

A human angles touch I feel
Weather you are far or near
When your near your touch is real
When far its just as dear
Because I experience the
etherial

Love you
2-23-98   Bobbie

Office (360) 892-8913 • FAX (360) 892-2636
7710 NE Vancouver Mall Drive • Vancouver, Washington 98662

IVORY
Like Carved IVORY
and as pure of mind
thoughtful and Kind
Eyes that can shine
Jean forever mine Bobby
12-12-98

I Love Jean from top
to bottom.
My mind and heart
she has gotten.

Bobby
12-11-98

To Me

So sweet to me you seem
That at times I faint my eyes
And they shed tears of joy
At the corners of my nose
As they trickle to my lips
With saltyness so sweet
Then with a short breath or two
A gentle chest tightness grows
Then again I return to reality
Because you are still next to me
Filling the air with ecstasy
  For me!

  Bobby 8-15-98

Buckle up relax.
Love ya still but deep.

Jean

My dearest being.
Fragile as a butterfly.
Sweet as nectar pie.
Not unlike a dove,
Docile and full of love.
Don't cry dear thing.
You are a fine human being.
Too soft is your heart.
Until death you depart.
Inner peace for you I pray.
Hope you find some one day.
  Soon
    1-10-99
   Bobby ♥ Jean
    in love you

Reverberations

A dark area in her head.
Reverberations incessantly
Caroms inside her mind.
Bounding side to side
For decades ricocheting
Ceasing not from year to year
One after the other
Nothing stops the malady
But don't you see as
you pray to God daily
Reason begs reality
Realize even grave
sinners from above
After a few words or so
Will recieve absolution
But not you.
Why not . Why not
You have earned peace.

  Bobby 6-4-98
  (cont'd)

Happy Birthday

Scotch party today
Law & Order to play
If its recorded okay
But I also must say
Love you the same way
  as yesterday
    Bobby 7-18-00

POEMS

Some are about love

Others cite beauty

Again there is duty
   or
Possibly all the above

Ode to ones loyal wife

Standing by through strife

Which I hold so dear

That death I need not fear

For tranquility is near

How fine its been

Fulfilled compleatly

   As I am.

Bobby
7-13-1999

Too Late

Right or wrong it
shouldn't be.
That anything comes
between you and me.
My sorrow is deep
and married to my mind
Like other similar times
   Deeply etched
   Painfully clear
   Pardon me
   Oh one that
   I hold so dear
Sealed with a Tear   Bobby
                            2-26-00

Also

Older now its clear
   also
Time together is more dear
   also
Because we grew so near
   also
Easier now to melancoley Tears
   also
Love you more it seems to appear
   also
No more do I fear
     Love
      Bobby
        10-31-99
        10:12:55

Older Now

The 70ties are here
and we are still near.
I am more quiet now
Don't say love you enough
Even though its not tough.
Think of your eyes when no word
Nothing needs to be said
Dimmer now because of pain
I consider that as a shame
I hope I am not to blame
As I sit with a heavy chest
   and
Will try my very best
To show more interest
and give my ass less rest
        Bobbie 7-6-00

Pray

My love you see
Is so dear to me
She is not pain free
Hurts are too many
But her heart a plenty
When happy her glow
Her eyes do it show
Then happyness is mine
But when she is down
In tears my eyes drown
And in my gloom
Fearing what is to come.
Pray!

10-20-00
Bobby

Just Because

I love you
Simple as that.

Bobby

Autry's 4 Seasons Florist

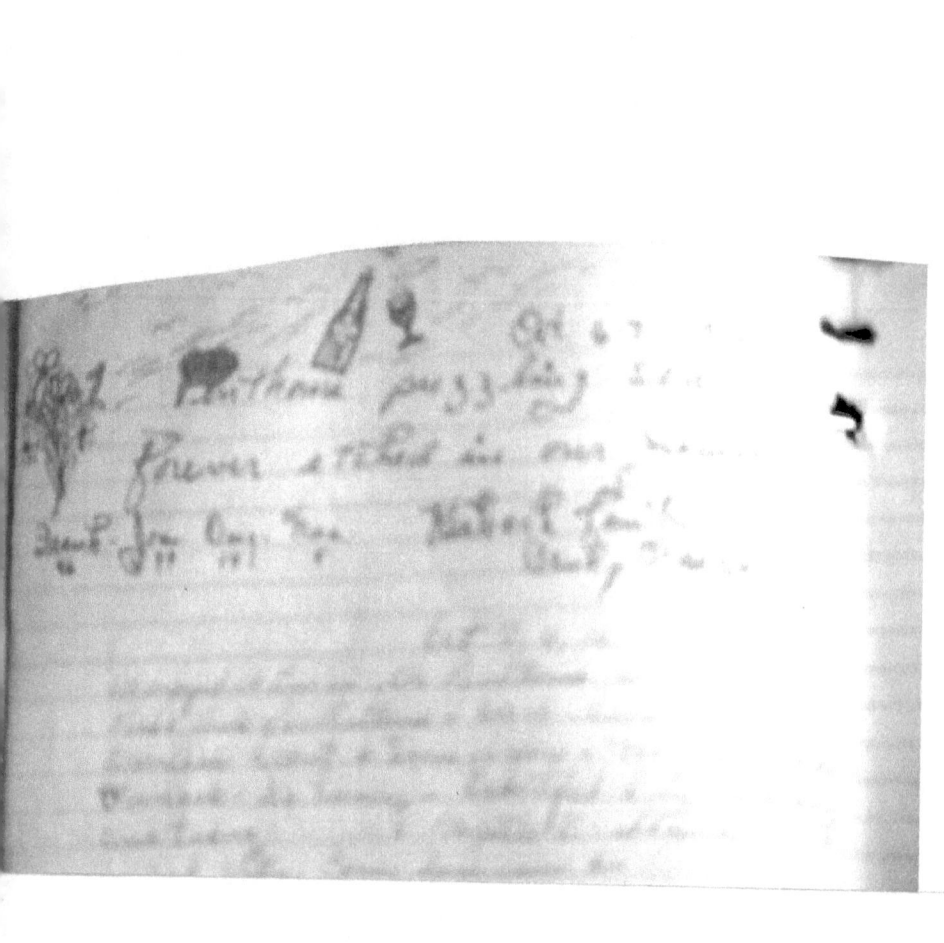

Ted and Vann
Donn and Joy
et al

Dec. 7th   8.9⁰⁰ 1972

#2

Sunset shining moon scimitar
above the southern horizon.
Two leagues below a solitary star.
Mark an established high
Record low outside suffered by
a fine log fire brandy coffee
A rarity indeed a coast full of snow
at zero and below.
Once but nare again will we
see it so. (from the Penthouse)
                Frank & Joan Kukuck
                    Bend, Oregon.

SCIMITAR 2 SP
SIMITAR NO
SYMITAR MIDEAST

Charles + Helen Bruemmer

11· 16·17·18· 1973   #3

Met with the bunch from the south and east.
Set up in the Penthouse along with the eights.
Were told there was a big Gale on the way
         Tapped the big keg - Drank
Toasting ourselves and the big one above
Lost the femmes early another at two but
the big "L's" stayed up till four
    Enjoying pour after pour
Crippled by quenched thirst awoke at mid A.M.
        Was sunny and bright
        The Gale didn't show
So but a peaceful beach under the blue.
    It's strength thundered through
    Detoxified refreshed restored.

Toast to Lynn.   Frank & Joan Kukuck

Nov 27, 28-29-30 — Travis + Jean Lake in # 8
& Nora too —
Came in the sun
Left in the rain.
Hell of a Holiday
once again — $18.75
No time to
pen my usual refrains.

Dec 5, 6, 7, 1975

Stormy weekend. Had dinner at Lincoln House with
David and Bonnie Jeffers, meet people who own "5.

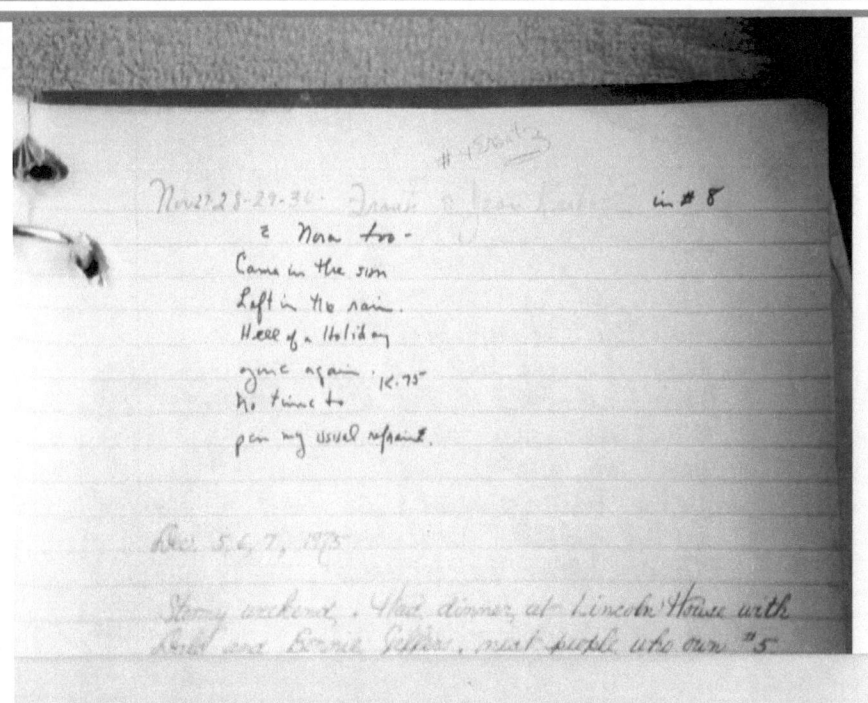

decided to stay until today (Tuesday) Oct 5th
Ted + Vern —

Oct 9-89. At times we can't get the penthouse for sale
so we accept something on another floor still
full pleasure galore —

Oct 9th sunny out 80° with a smile breeze
Stay 04 through a newly painted penthouse door
back to you we desire the empty rooms
better you see the Siding
Rick & Audrey # 5188
Anese 1962 (Rib. Nan 63)
We take the morning — Or Ted & Vern
If Lynn is back let us know — if you
want to sell a slice of the pie
we are always with them touts in penalty
Kirkov + Randi

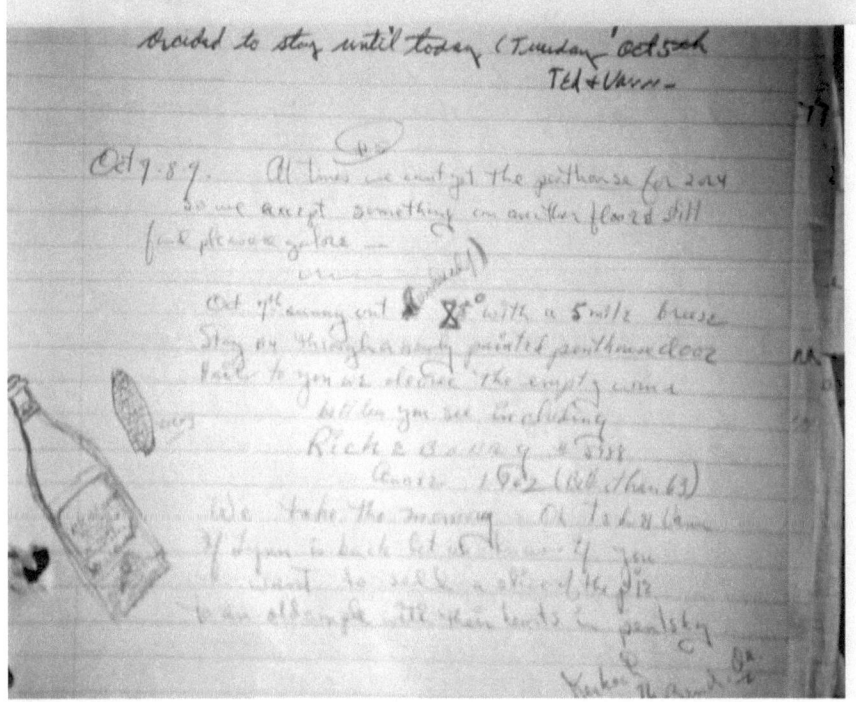

Feb 7 – 9:00 PM Tide Out
Alone than three descend
One hundred steps to a
Night time quiet beach.
Above two stars shine through
thin whisps of air suspended dew
Along are lights up on the hills
Both filtered through trees and dew
50° No wind at all
Oceans white cresting waves - move
Four - five at a time ever smaller
toward shore while up on the hill
Smoke columns move straight up
Are they
Fingers of praise to one above K-77
  Richard # 5

It misted yesterday morning and this morning the sun is warm and friendly. Such are the vagaries of Oregon weather!

Janet Norling, Vancouver, Wn.
Shirley Iff

— GULLS ARE STILL EVERYWHERE

Sept. 22-24, 1986 - #7 - #6 VISIT 1976 - #1 VISIT 1972 PLEASE SEE OLD BOOK

The long hiatus made us return
Bade us
Retire to the sea and be happy
 momentarily
Notice — one thing you cant see
 is a palm tree
So here are three from me
 to thee.

O.K. ("HELLO" IN OUR GUEST BOOK)   KERKOCH - 1985 - 9-27
 BEND, OR

With a melancholy
Tear or two
 and by Jove
Hi Lynn Liff on
 wife

To celebrate our prior
 pleasant memories
 of Previous Stays —
We popped the cork
 of a bottle or two —
And drank them
 toasting the good old
 days. Pasted the label of one
 on the opposite page hoping to
 review it on other sunny days.
          K. 85.

Gud
Välsigna

Two Sided Poems

For Silence

The children are asleep
a fires crack is all I hear
On this night so deep and still.
I think about our quiet life
and wonder why beneath my
breast all thoughts lie dead.
Where is this match I seek.
I speak all day and much
at night but my dreams of
    you all lie unsaid.
Why so mute with tender phrases
- pure love - happiness - content - and more
when I feel the pleasure of there glow.
Could they if told lead to a fatal
    blow — no
But none will flow because of
of some tight unseen band
whichisabout my chest. This
thing that I cannot explain.
I hope this paradox is mine
alone and locks on others breasts
are burned away as words
unfold for lovers to behold.

Lined up a place to eat
Both Hoff Street. Sounded neat.
But the din - did me in
Before I ordered my first round.
Retreat the Ambassador
as I walked by seemed neat.
Rear, Palm room one
look around nostalgia
abound - was a place for us
a cocktail or two - before
a dinner you see.
The view at 82 was of
palms inside and out
Blooming flowers abound
missed you not around.
So had a martini
c̄ twist & olive too
Took a look around not a
couple lades in around.
Ambassador Lantare 7:30
Believe it or not empty
save for me - and a serenad
to private party.

5-5-82

BURNS #2 But can you read it.

I ordered a full carafe for myself, but found it is enough for two or at least 1½. Ordered the T-Bone not chicken cuz you weren't there. Didn't notice had the smell. But I must say – Big is the way.
> Found there was no big anyway. then I have only one hint.

Cut next to the bone a work your way out on the M.bg. side. Leave the rest for the dogs outside. Made it early Done by 7:30.. Crowd not as ~~tardy~~ sturdy – waitress still burly.

Looked over my shoulder was not sure But lo a behold he didn't appear

Dear Bill

for dessert or even the meal.

Plan to go to the Tavern for a beer and a cut of the cards if it will be.

Found one thing for sure Boyds deceit beats Sankas forever and a year. – Carry it and a deg ~~et~~

Hot water my dear.

I only hope you agree for I love you – SEE. nevertheless in Burns its the dumbest K crowd we even espy. 5-5-82 to bed it was not 83

(Boyds is better I will get you some to carry)

Difference
Hard to understand
Harder to learn
Each marching to
  their own band.
Our face others harm
Escaping the light and
Others ways are hard to
        grasp
Like hand fulls of dry
       sand.
In time one begins to see
at [...] everyone on
   [...]
But if love is a partner
    in the battle
                  (over)

Does it really matter?
       No!
     Sequence
  Minor consequence
  No real difference.
      Love Bobby K
        5-20-91

Four Seasons
Hotels·Resorts

Reverberations

A dark area in her head.
Reverabations incesently
Caroms inside her mind.
Bounding side to side
For decades rickoshaying
Ceasing not from year to year
One after the other
Nothing stops the malody
But dont you see as
you pray to God daily
Reason begs reality
Realize even grave
sinners from above
after a few words or so
will recieve absolution
But not you.
Why not, why not
You have earned peace.

Bobby
6.4.98

Forgive yourself. God has more than 10,000 times and I haven't because I don't think you have done wrong.

A Day

Sunny A.M. on Baptism Day
As Todd an Liz spends
a morning at play
Breakfast served in a leasurely way.
Todd & Doug go out to play
While Joan puts dishes away
Every one scrubbed then in
finery dressed
Out to the chapel we Trek
As all the others are met.
Ceremony follows as the prayer
words the principles say.
With water cleansing all sins away
Peacefully recongrate n 9th st.
Before we all meet ngaints est

The lunch was jolly and long
With wine food and good cheer
No arguements here
Every one departs ~~to~~ ~~the~~ Travels back
~~Hope~~
  Good luck as all return home
To end an unforgetable Day

Rough draft
Fagottere of Rediscovered
12-8-96
D. Do not show Bobby
N Jean because of the
connections

Photos

Author

Cheryl Krkoč

The End

Bibliography

Webster's New World Dictionary, College Edition
Copyright 1968 and 1953,1954,1956, 1957,1958,1959,1960,19
62,1964,1966 by
THE WORLD PUBLISHING COMPANY

The American Century Dictionary
Edited by Laurence Urdang
Warner Books Edition
Copyright 1995 by Oxford University Press, Inc.

The American Century Thesaurus
Laurence Urdang
Warner Books Edition
Copyright Laurence Urdang, Inc. 1992,1995,1996.

www.ingramcontent.com/pod-product-compliance
Lightning Source LLC
Chambersburg PA
CBHW021422070526
44577CB00001B/18